Adler Speaks

Adler Speaks

The Lectures of Alfred Adler

Compiled and Edited by
Mark H. Stone
and
Karen A. Drescher

iUniverse, Inc.
New York Lincoln Shanghai

Adler Speaks
The Lectures of Alfred Adler

All Rights Reserved © 2004 by Karen Drescher and Mark Stone

No part of this book may be reproduced or transmitted in any form or by any means, graphic, electronic, or mechanical, including photocopying, recording, taping, or by any information storage retrieval system, without the written permission of the publisher.

iUniverse, Inc.

For information address:
iUniverse, Inc.
2021 Pine Lake Road, Suite 100
Lincoln, NE 68512
www.iuniverse.com

ISBN: 0-595-31144-X

Printed in the United States of America

Contents

Introduction vii
Editorial Remarks ix
CHAPTER 1   The Science of Individual Psychology 1
CHAPTER 2   Individual Psychology and Freudian Psychology 10
CHAPTER 3   A Brief Comparison of Individual Psychology and Psychoanalysis 19
CHAPTER 4   Scientific Study of Character 22
CHAPTER 5   Courage 30
CHAPTER 6   Bashfulness 37
CHAPTER 7   Finicky Eating 42
CHAPTER 8   Laziness 46
CHAPTER 9   Mistakes of Childhood 48
CHAPTER 10   School Problems 50
CHAPTER 11   Stuttering 54
CHAPTER 12   Adolescence 58
CHAPTER 13   The Approach to Womanhood 61
CHAPTER 14   The Approach to Manhood 64
CHAPTER 15   Future of Love 67
CHAPTER 16   The Family Life 71

Chapter 17	Anxious Parents	77
Chapter 18	The Importance of Mother in Family and Social Life	80
Chapter 19	The Influence of the Father	86
Chapter 20	Migraine	91
Chapter 21	The Problem of Crime	94
Chapter 22	The Problem of Death	101
Chapter 23	Psychological Aspects in a Time of Economic Crisis	106
References and Additional Reading		109
Index		113

Introduction

Alfred Adler, (1875—1937) founder of Individual Psychology, introduced himself to the American public by embarking on a lecture tour in 1926. He spoke in major cities, at hospitals, churches, synagogues, schools, colleges and universities. Many of these speaking engagements have been transcribed and are held at the Library of Congress. While visiting the Library of Congress, Karen Drescher located the transcripts. With the goal of making these speeches available to those interested in learning more about Individual Psychology, Mark Stone and Karen Drescher have carefully selected transcripts dating from 1926 through 1933 to be included in this volume.

As a contribution to Individual Psychology, the editors are pleased to offer these lectures of Alfred Adler as a supplement to his published books and papers. They are modest in comparison to the rest of his written work. All of the speeches are in harmony with the mainstream tenets of Individual Psychology and corroborate what we already know about Adler's theories. At times they offer a slightly different slant on familiar topics.

It is interesting to observe that Adler used varying expressions for the same idea as he conveyed the principles of Individual Psychology. He reminds us to avoid fixating upon dogma. In the second speech Adler encourages us to think independently and find new ways of explaining his ideas. Adler gives us the clear message that we are not to take every word he used as the only means of explaining Individual Psychology.

Editorial Remarks

Introductions and editorial comments are printed in italics. Adler's words are printed in a standard font. A short commentary highlighting the points we consider essential follows each of the lectures. A list of references for additional reading is provided after the last chapter.

Every effort has been made to retain Adler's exact words, but this was not always possible in every instance. Sometimes words were missing from the transcript or words seemed incorrect. In a few places we substituted more contemporary words, but made such changes rarely, preferring to remind the reader that more than 60 years have passed since these lectures were given. Over time, words change their meaning and connotation. This needs to be taken into account when judging Adler's remarks. Alfred Adler was considered an excellent public speaker and lecturer. This is especially notable for a person lecturing in a second language. Ashley Montagu (1970) wrote these remarks:

"Adler's lecture, which was given to a full auditorium of students, was a revelation to me. It was extraordinarily impressive. I found myself most excited by the ideas which seemed to flow so effortlessly from the speaker. I don't think I had ever been quite as stirred by anyone before. While English was not his native tongue, Adler spoke with verve and fluency. It was a virtuoso performance in every way. I had heard many good speakers in my time, and of them all perhaps Bernard Shaw was the best, but Adler was much mightier. I would now say that Adler was among the two or three best speakers I have ever heard." (p. 17).

The only film segment of Alfred Adler delivering a speech clearly validates Montagu's appraisal. Adler speaks with a Viennese accent, but delivered his message in faultless English. (See www.sc.edu/newsfilm).

The editors wish to acknowledge Bernard Knauer, Sybil Mandell and all of the other individuals who transcribed Alfred Adler's speeches. We also wish to acknowledge Alan Porter for his collaborative work with Dr. Adler in London. We are especially grateful to Alexandra, Kurt and Margot Adler for making these archival materials available through the Library of Congress.

1

The Science of Individual Psychology

This lecture was given at Temple Emanuel in New York City on 5 November 1929. Adler's use of the phrase "a gay science" may derive from the title of a work by Nietzsche who wanted science to be an adventure of discovery. The word "gay" appears to have a similar meaning for Adler.

I feel greatly honored to lecture to you on my subject, Individual Psychology. In this lecture I will explain what we have accomplished in our science. The demands of education are really the same in all kinds of schools. Education is always expected to teach a child to be a good person and a good citizen. Now we have had to go still further to find out the reasons why so many children and also adults could not find the right way, could not educate themselves, or could not be educated.

In order to make progress along these lines we have to distinguish two parts in regard to our inquiries. The first part includes these questions: "What is expressed?" "What do we want later in life?" "For which questions and problems should we be treated?" Therefore, we have had to look at our life, and ask ourselves the question, "What is the meaning of life?" You know this question is the same question as you find in all the religions and in politics and in our social life, and so on. We do not wish to replace any of these movements in our work. We want to contribute. We want to add to what we find.

If I ask, "What is the meaning of life?" You could answer, as a very wise man has answered, "If you do not ask me I know it, but if you ask me I do not know it." It is really not so simple to answer this one question. Upon closer examination, we find that all of us answer this question by our conduct, however inarticulate we may be, in formulating the answer in words. For instance, a man who wants to commit suicide says in his actions, "The meaning in life is nothing for me, there is no meaning." Many wise people have answered it in the same way.

If you ask troubled children, the children who cry and tyrannize their whole environment, "What is the meaning of life?" they will probably say, "To be a good kid." If you look at the movements and expressions of these children, you will find that their meaning in life is to be the boss, to get everything that they want.

Insane individuals want to be the highest, on top, emperor or empress, king or queen. Criminals have a very clear meaning in life, that is, to satisfy their own desire and never mind others. Drunkards want to escape and have an easy release. This is the meaning of life as they express it. Sexual perverts also have their meaning of life. They justify their life in this way because for them "drives" rule the world.

To say that everyone expresses their own meaning of life is not enough. This explanation does not satisfy us. It is not easy to express it in simple words. Therefore, I would like to make a detour. This detour can be made only if you are on the right track. If we could fancy that we are immortal and nothing could be a danger for us, and we are not vulnerable in any way, then life would not have a meaning. We could do anything that we wished.

A belief in an immortal life may profoundly influence our movements. But even with the belief in immortality we still are not satisfied, we wish to improve and to improve within the short time allotted to us. We desire improvement not for ourselves alone, but for the whole human race. Life is a continuing process. As we work out the pattern of our individual lives in our actions each of us evolves our own meaning of life.

The meaning of life must be created by each individual. We must not be presented with it. It would not work if we were presented with it. We have to strive for it. We have to understand and act and work in this way and determine what this means for the future. This means for the whole of society, and for cooperation in the present time and in the future. If you have this one clue, you will find that everything we judge in our life is formed in accordance with the degree of cooperation. How do we understand what it means, how do we approach it, identify and cooperate with another person? When we speak, we cooperate. When we listen, we cooperate. Everything we call good, right, worthwhile, or normal is called and distinguished in this way.

I wish to make a distinction, cooperation is understood as social adjustment. Social interest is a great part of what determines the meaning of life. On this point is focused all the efforts made by an adaptable person in this world. Now you see in many ways, how this resembles the views of many, the great efforts made and developed in the history of the human race. "Love your neighbor" was much earlier in the hearts, on the tongue and in the heads of human beings.

Often in our life we do not know that we have to cooperate, and we do not know why, but we see it. We started from this point, and I could insist there is no virtue in this world that would not be a virtue arising from cooperation. All the good characteristics are those of cooperation: to be good, to be true, faithful, brave, courageous and to be optimistic. They signify cooperation.

All the little and big problems of life are social problems and demand cooperation and a preparation. These are the problems of family life, and this I will describe in another lecture. We must look at the reaction of the child toward the father, the mother, toward other children. We must also observe the child's relation to friends, how the child enters school, how the child approaches schoolwork, if the child aspires to be a good pupil, and the child's willingness to cooperate.

Later in life, the problem of comradeship is always an expression of an interest in others. It is always the result of a certain degree of cooperation. Our whole life is involved with this great power, which has forced the human race to take part in the life of each other. It means cooperation, and, therefore, it occupies a very important part in understanding the meaning of life. It is also part of the relation to the other sex, and the problems of sex, love and marriage. It always means cooperation. It means How to be interested in the other person." This makes clear the goals toward which we will educate our children. As these goals become clear, we see that the major task before us is directing our energies toward finding a way that these goals may be achieved. This requires applying the principles of Individual Psychology. When we talk about cooperating with another person, it does not always mean that this other person will cooperate.

In education we can often find the good will of the parents and teachers, even so the child resists. Therefore, it is not only necessary to know all the means and tools for education, or have all the instruments, pictures and books, it means much more. It means knowing in which dangerous corners the influence of education can be hampered. Also, it requires knowing why some children are not prepared correctly for this kind of cooperation. Above everything else, it must be known, where the mistakes are made. Individual Psychology, so far as I can see in the past thirty years, has found the roots of these mistakes as to why children cannot cooperate.

Cooperation is the most important thing for living. To explain it, I must show you the important progress made by Individual Psychology in emphasizing the unity of the mind of an individual. It is not possible that in the mind of an individual there are two different tracks. It must always be unity. Parts of an individual produce coherence only when combined as a whole. In the growth and development of the body there must be an ideal of form toward which the body and mind grow. We know the ideal form of an individual body. The ideal for a human body is always the desire to create unity to a certain degree. If you cut off the skin, it will grow together because something is leading it.

If we ask, in a scientific manner, why skin grows together we will say because life wants to be continued, but if we inquire as to the causation of life, at the same time, I am looking at the striving for an ideal form. This means that we can underrate the growth of body and mind only from the future, only from the finish, only from the final act toward which a person is striving in the development of the body and the mind. In regards to the body, we do not know very much, and the influence of the individual is really very small, but in regard to mind, we are discovering much more.

We can understand the creative power which enables us to change, but understanding comes to us only when we take into consideration that the goal of all the potentialities brought in this world by a new born child is always influenced and stimulated by striving toward a goal which will help the child overcome difficulties. Striving to overcome difficulties goes to the end, to find the goal of superiority in a vague manner. In this way, as you see, you have a goal of superiority toward which you can lead all your potentialities, to arouse feelings and emotions not only those belonging to the present, but those belonging to the future, in spite of the fact that nothing has changed.

We are living upon the earth's crust, yet we see a future in which we expect to overcome all the difficulties of this life. We are really arousing feelings and emotions. We could understand these as optimistic feelings and emotions. From these feelings and emotions, we develop a new power to go on in a better way. We stimulate ourselves in this way to look for a better future. We look for the improvement of an individual and for the improvement of the whole human race.

In this connection I want to mention that we are dreaming. We are dreaming in our daily life, every hour of every day. These dreams are no different from the dreams in sleep, where we arouse feelings and emotions, grasping them out of the air only for the purpose of enlarging and enforcing our feelings and emotions to make them stronger than before. In this way, we strive even more for the goal of superiority. If you understand that this striving for unity arouses problems and questions, and does so in a cooperative manner, then you will see that this must fit into the welfare of the whole human race.

The key to Individual Psychology is to find the degree of an individual's ability for cooperation. Individuals striving for superiority meet the greatest difficulties when they want to solve the social problems of friendship, love, work, and they are not prepared. Therefore, we must look for their interest in cooperating, if they are interested. Many of the mistakes that are made are done so because people are not rightly prepared for the social tasks that arise in life.

When we look back we find that children are born in a different state of body. Some of them are more mature, and some suffer imperfections. The environment plays a role in the way individuals develop. Difficulties form and create their movements and their expressions. Imperfect organs burden a child, and the more the child experiences feelings of insecurity, the more the child will make use of this weakness.

The more a human being suffers and feels burdened, the more the individual will strive to be rid of and overcome difficulties. The individual strives toward a goal of superiority with every inherent ability. Because they are suffering, we can understand why these children are more interested in immediate success. Therefore, they develop characteristics of impatience. They loose interest in others and become more interested in themselves. They develop egotistical characteristics or feel that they are in danger. This can be avoided. These children can be saved from being egotistical, but a certain method must be used. Education is required to help relieve these feelings. Many grow up with a great feeling of inferiority, always seeking easier ways to cooperate, and always looking out for themselves.

We cannot force children to answer as we want. If we give children a chance of success in a useful way when they enter school, for instance, success in mathematics, writing, or drawing, they will excel. If we do not give them a chance, many children will become discouraged and stop their interest. Why should we judge the gift of the child? If children are not prepared, what can we do? We must give children a chance of success.

I want to extinguish the superstition of inheritance. I believe that Individual Psychology made the first effort to extinguish it. Later John Watson went the same way. We are very glad to have a collaborator in this field. It is very clear and obvious to everybody who is not narrowly focused in this field. I have hinted that these imperfect organs are inherited, but we know the difficulties from these inherited imperfect organs can be extinguished; therefore, inheritance is not important. It is only important to find the right method for how to help these children.

You will find that every child suffers from a feeling of inferiority. Therefore, each child can be destroyed if the development of cooperation is neglected. You need only arrange a simple situation in which a nearly normal child develops the same as a child born with imperfect organs. If you contaminate the food and air, you have the same suffering as those who suffer from imperfect lungs. You can infect perfect children with TB and they will suffer in the same way as those who suffer from imperfect organs resulting from heredity. Unfortunately, we have not gone very far in this area, but here is a broad field for inquiries, and for research in dealing with their improvement.

Children suffering from imperfect organs, like all children, strive for personal superiority. Their striving is blocked because they always meet social problems and they respond with discouragement about their ability to achieve what is expected. They are not guilty. We find this lack of cooperation in all of the fields of life.

We find a lack of cooperation in the problem child, the neurotic, criminals, suicides, drunkards and sexual perverts. All of these individuals express a low degree of cooperation. In this way they are alike. They are not alike in the degree to which they limit their activity. Each of them has a different sphere of activity. When we look at their degree of activity, we see that a lack of cooperation is always visible.

Children must avoid this great feeling of inferiority because it only makes a child self-centered. If we look further, we find another situation in which a child becomes self-centered. These are the pampered, petted children. These children are wholly dependent upon one person and develop as life's parasites. They expect everything and are not trained in giving. They always want to be the centers of attention, and develop egotistical characteristics such as impatience and so on. They are very emotional. If they miss something that they want, they become upset. They are trained to be with the one person who pampers them. They want to get rid of all the other persons with whom they are not connected. When asked to look or listen they will not cooperate.

All types of imperfections are dependent upon the lack of cooperation. When they meet the social problems later in life, they are in such great tension that they suffer physically. They will be irritated, and neurotic symptoms will arise. They are looking for easier ways to be the center of attention. Individual Psychology has identified a specific diagnosis of the pampered child, a child whose behavior is unceasing.

Another very important point which has been stressed by Individual Psychology and agrees with the findings of others is that the most important impressions which form and mold the unity and style of life of a child are those made in the first four or five years of life. This time is wholly sufficient to fix this pattern and these patterns will not be changed. The pattern is like a finished unity. Striving continues and develops toward a certain individual interest, and everything is oriented toward this interest. That main interest is personal superiority without cooperation.

We must also consider the child who feels hated. This child has not developed the ability to cooperate. Therefore, later in life the child usually fails. Children are composed of all types. A greater part of the individuals who fail in life are individuals experiencing discouragement, feelings of inferiority and lack interest in cooperating.

Do you understand the necessity for the skill of the mother? She has to do this work. She is the first person in the child's life who strives for an ever increasing ability for cooperation between mother and child. She is integral in helping the child expand this interest toward others. The next chapter in this story is that the father must contribute, to assist in developing the child's ability to cooperate.

We must also consider the social environment of the child. If this environment is a hostile environment, and if we find hatred and great difficulties, anxiety and so on, it can be understood how these social factors also influence a child because they influence the parents and the whole family life. On this point I want to say that cooperation does not mean just a word or notion, it means an attitude. It means a certain amount of optimism, with feelings and emotions operating in the same way, a way that is interested in others. We must not believe that the individual could not be damaged or forgotten. If I want to cooperate, I must bring myself to such a position that I will be able to cooperate. This individual will be saved. When individuals look only for their own interests, then they cannot develop the ability of cooperation.

Altruism is real cooperation. It is the right way. Individualism is a mistake if it is only for one's own development. We also see that optimism is a goal of superiority on the useful side of life. Therefore, optimism is the right way, and pessimism is the wrong way. Optimistic dreams arouse feelings and emotions that look for a happy ending and help dreamers collect their powers. Even when failure occurs, they will try and go on again. Pessimists are lacking this view. They are not backed by their feelings and emotions. On the contrary, they are hindered. When they meet difficulties and fail, they say they knew it would happen, but they do not know that they have created this defeat.

On this point you will see that Individual Psychology is a very optimistic science and a gay science. We do not believe that there are not ways in which we think we cannot overcome difficulties. About this attack on heredity, you will hear more, but what I want to say is that after four or five years a pattern and style of life are created lacking cooperation for what must be done later. We have to find the right institutions to support what must be done later. Child Guidance Clinics, for instance, can help when failure is apparent, or after problems occur. But this is often too late. We should have institutions that could begin much earlier. They should be connected with the schools. In our public schools and in private schools in which we meet children, it is very easy to find out which child has not accomplished the ability to cooperate.

Someday the well-taught teacher will understand these matters and will know how to avoid mistakes. Later, they will learn how to treat children and how to make them more cooperative. We have to act as we do with other subjects. If children fail in arithmetic, what is to be done? They must be prepared better for arithmetic. If they fail in cooperation, they must be prepared for cooperation. How can we prepare a person for better cooperation? This point must be discussed.

I want to mention that Individual Psychology has shown great progress. We believe that we are able to explain to a child who has failed that the child is lacking cooperation so that this child will also understand it, but we must explain it in an artistic way. We cannot preach; we cannot do it in that way. We must impress the child. The child must hear expressions not heard before. Therefore, we must look for ways to succeed, and we must begin with infants. We must encourage and help children to cooperate with us.

Encouraging children is an art. I have stressed methods that are found mostly on the keyboard of Individual Psychology. You must learn to play this keyboard. This is the art of Individual Psychology. When I look back on what I would like to describe as the main contribution of Individual Psychology, I would say it is having the right understanding of the importance of cooperation. The science of life, the meaning of life, always demands cooperation.

I would also like to mention this point: children suffer in different ways from feelings of inferiority and they want to compensate for these feelings. The greatest feelings of inferiority are seen when an individual develops a strong feeling of superiority and lacks ability for cooperation. These individuals develop egotistic abilities. We must address this lack of cooperation. We must find other points of view, a better diagnosis, a view that is found in the science of Individual Psychology.

We know how to change this pattern if we go back and convince the child that the child created a mistaken way of thinking and interacting with others. This child does not have to create in this way. If the child does not understand, we do not punish or scold or suppress or use authority. We explain in ways we are sure will help. Then we have made great progress.

Commentary:

When Adler says, "The meaning of life must be created by each individual" he provides a clear indication of the fundamental task facing every person. Everybody must make their own way. Later, we note that this life-task can be divided into the subtasks of work, friendship and love that are frequently referred to as if there are three life-tasks. As we consider this point we are reminded by Adler that personality is unified, and not to be divided. We have a single function as we live our life upon "the earth's crust," and that is to create a sense of meaning for living. How we do that belies our interpretation of our own self, others, and the world around us.

Adler reminds us that we have the creative power. We make what we will of any situation. We create perceptions of ourselves and everything that happens, and act as if those perceptions were accurate. This interpretation becomes what is known as Life Style. Life Style embodies all that we are in the present, think we were in the past and plan to become in the future. It is formed unwittingly unless we are remarkably insightful. Therefore, we usually require some outside assistance by which to guide self-investigations. Understanding one's Life Style is akin to self-discovery, but with more emphasis upon recognizing the "hidden goal" that often lies at the base, and governs most of what we think and do. Recognizing this hidden, fictive goal to which we strive, provides the key to understanding who we are.

Our goal is to overcome life's challenges, to achieve superiority, i.e. to be superior in all we do. As we strive to meet life's challenges, we ought not to make that movement an incessant drive to conquer all. Adler tells us that the key to Individual Psychology is social interest. He encourages us to strive in socially useful ways. According to Adler, all of life's challenges are social challenges requiring cooperation. He encourages us to meet these challenges with expressions of social interest. Some individuals confuse cooperation with compliance. Compliance infers obedience, submission or acquiescence. This is not what Adler was intending. When he used the word cooperation he was talking about collaborative efforts. Each person pitches in, each person takes the risk of contributing. Adler promoted a sense of optimism about the human race and our ability to handle life.

2

Individual Psychology and Freudian Psychology

This lecture was given on 4 December 1930. We do not know the occasion or place. Adler compares his views to those of Freud, especially concerning the issues of drives and the unconscious.

Individual Psychology is an ambitious endeavor. I thank the group for their contributions. They have undertaken a considerable task. Individual Psychology is not a conceited science. We do not believe we have spoken the last word. We make this great effort because we can contribute to the welfare of the human family. In this striving, we meet all the sciences. Science is worthwhile because it is looking for the truth, and to look for the truth always means to make a contribution. The scientific meaning of life is contribution.

Relative to other schools of psychology, I will explain my own interpretations. I will also illustrate the great differences between Individual Psychology and Psychoanalysis. In America there is greater confusion over my position than there is in Europe. In America, individuals studying psychology have been trained and are accustomed to calling each school of psychology 'psychoanalysis.' In Europe, psychoanalysis refers only to the Freudian school of psychology. This is what I would like to explain.

This school and this science of psychology were explained more than thirty years ago. I will not interpret the meanings of any collaborators. It is astonishing to discover that in this school, only Freud has moved forward; the others have followed. In Individual Psychology it is different. I would not want to be leading, while the others only agree with everything I have described. I do not want my collaborators to use the same words and notions. It is better for them to think independently and to find new ways of explanation because I am now fixed in my meanings and notions which can be misunderstood and are misunderstood. This is especially true when someone does not know the whole meaning of the science of Individual Psychology. They may pick out one little part. If I were to describe the great work of Freud, I may make the same mistake in regard to Psychoanalysis.

When I was a young student and a medical man, I was worried and discontented with the state of psychiatry. I tried to find other ways and I found Freud. He was courageous enough to go another way, and to find the importance of psychic reasons for bodily disturbances and for the neuroses. This had been in doubt by some authors, especially the French. As psychoanalysis evolved, I have seen some ideas that made sense and some ideas that were not in agreement with common sense, nor have they agreed with important views of psychology and psychiatry. In my striving to find a better way I was often in dispute with Freud and his collaborators.

I am positive that I have never presented a psychological principle that I have not experienced myself. This has been the strength and power of Individual Psychology. As I discovered, every part agrees with all the other parts. I saw the marvelous harmony of the style of life. Yet, Freud was pointing out strongly the science of sexual psychology and the sexual libido. This was at the time when he was only interested in the notion that every movement, every expression, and symptom had a sexual factor. Freud insisted culture resulted from the suppression of the sexual libido. He was determined to develop this line of thinking. However, many other psychological factors must be considered. I quickly discovered that a libido and a sexual drive are without direction. I also discovered a view in which I could find coherence. This is the most important part of Individual Psychology.

Aggression is an attitude toward life. I have understood with great experience and with many proofs that this attitude toward life is seen in all movements and symptoms. Freud and his followers adopted this idea of aggression. Yet, they conformed to an old line of thinking and explained aggression as an inherited attitude toward the external life that was bad, hostile, and sadistic. This is how Freud arrived at the idea of drive psychology.

Freud insisted that drives always need to be satisfied. Yet, drives are without direction. How will they satisfy this desire? Is there only one way to satisfy a drive? Freud, I am sure, was greatly influenced by Nietzsche who tells us 'each pleasure wants eternity.' If you grasped Nietzsche's meaning, you have grasped a great part of Freudian Psychoanalysis. What would happen if drives could not be satisfied? What if drives did not follow the pleasure principle?

According to Freud, drives are not simple. Drives have a brain, a mind, attitudes, feelings and understanding. Drives incorporate both ego and personality. Drives know what to do if suppressed; they work from the unconscious. On this point I understood what Freud accomplished. He arrived at the idea that drives are suppressed by our cultured life. On this point, an interesting thing happened. I discovered the mistake. Freud insisted that culture derives from suppressed sexual drives. He went on to say that sexual drives are suppressed by our culture. These two ideas cannot agree with each other. Freud helped himself in a funny way. When he was asked about the incongruence, he answered: 'What came first, the chicken or the egg?' It was a poor answer. In Individual Psychology if you use a metaphor, you have to have something in mind. You escape otherwise.

I saw more than Freud did regarding drives as a principal factor in the mind and psyche. Long ago a German philosopher said 'the drive develops the personality.' The philosopher did not mean that the drive as Freud conceived of it was beyond the ego; the philosopher meant that the drive becomes the ego. Freud calls it the 'id' and believes it extends beyond all limits of body and mind. According to Freud, the id creates all the other components: the ego, superego, cultured ego, the ideal ego, the censor, all expressions and movements. The battle between the unconscious (created by the id) and the ego (also created by the id) is responsible for neurotic symptoms. This could not be seen, but there is some logic to Freud's thinking.

When individuals are not able to meet life's challenges, they display neurotic symptoms because the cultured ego resists healthy approaches to life's challenges. Following this logic, Freud had to explain why so many persons hindered by culture, develop neurotic symptoms. Freud insisted that all drives created by the id are inherited in different qualities and quantities. The inheritance is responsible for suppression which in turn leads to neurotic symptoms. Suppression of drives is hard to explain. The suppression of drives and the unconscious can only be accomplished by means of a censor. Who created the censor? Does the censor control the whole work? There must be something different which leads, creates, and accomplishes.

Unlike Freud's school of psychology, Individual Psychology insists that nothing is found beyond the ego. Everything is ego. The ego cannot be grasped, and cannot be discovered in prenatal time. It is not seen on the baby's first day. The ego is growing, developing and striving for an ideal final form. Individual Psychology calls this 'finalism.' In the beginning formulation of the mind and the body, the final ideal is active, and always moving toward this final goal. All other considerations are futile. If this goal exists, with an ideal final form in mind and body, then as the mind develops, all inherited traits participate. Individuals make use of these traits in their own unique way.

Intelligence, feelings, actions and adaptations must be included in the growth of the ego so that the ego begins to create. When the ego is censored, persons can be in doubt about what is right and what is wrong. These persons may develop an ability to do the right thing, in which case, they will always resist the wrong. The censor is the ego, the style of life, and the creative power of each individual. Therefore, drives, super ego, the censor, and feelings of guilt are the creations of the ego. So far, in drive psychology, what we could never find out was why a drive develops in a certain line toward a certain goal, and why this drive has everything a thinking person has in mind.

In these concepts you can see how Freud liked to use mechanistic principles and a certain striving to press through and overpower the censor. He was completely entrenched in mechanistic thinking, and he used mechanistic principles to explain the psyche. It cannot be denied that Freud was attempting to make psychoanalysis a science. He tried to find an underlying, unifying idea to explain the differing immediate experiences of human life. He attempted to find a focus for all the differences. But Freud's principles did not apply to all the facts. Therefore, he wanted to have a substitute for the drives. He always had to say '...in addition...' and then find new factors, such as the 'Oedipus Complex.'

Freud's thoughts regarding the Oedipus complex were in terms of sexual libido and the development of sex. What Freud found was a pure and simple description of the sexual urge, but not sexual drives in specific forms. Each individual has a form of sexuality which agrees with the individual's personality. The sexual urge was a different part.

Freud attempted to explain differences in sexuality, not just sexual urges. He came to the conclusion that sexuality is found all over the body. Freud explained that in children sexuality is found at any aperture (eyes, mouth, ears, etc.) He believed that a child is born with widespread sexuality and that as the child develops normal sexuality arises. On this point, Freud wanted to explain the different forms of perversion. He pointed out that there are always resistive components. Freud found these resistive components in astonishingly tremendous numbers. Finally, he decided that everyone has a narcissistic tendency for sexuality. This meant that individuals wanted to satisfy sexual drives within their own bodies through masturbation.

Freud theorized that the inherited drive which involves the mouth has the potential to become a fixation. He tried to explain that eating was a sadistic act. Freud went on to explain that the first sadistic act performed by any individual is breast feeding. Freud emphasized the pleasure principle and labeled the activity of the drives, sadistic. On the other hand, Individual Psychology, always looking for contribution and cooperation, finds that breast-feeding is not a sadistic act, but an act of cooperation between mother and child. It is necessary that they work together.

Individual Psychology emphasizes the necessity for cooperation between mother and child. Individual Psychology explains that the child is dependent on the mother. This may be in a good way, or it may be in a bad way. In contrast, Freud indicated 'as the sexual libido develops, children, especially the boys, want to have a child by the mother, and they want to kill the father.' There are hints that some boys want their mothers in this way.

Aside from sexuality, there are boys who want to control and dominate their mothers. They always want to be accompanied by their mother. In some ways this desire is characteristic of a certain type of individual, especially in the sexual urge. A child may wish to have sexual relations with his mother, but this is rare. But for Freud, this is not rare.

When children do not wish to be left alone, they say 'ah, huh.' When children are afraid to be left alone and cry at night, they say 'ah, huh.' In this way, the child controls the mother by keeping her busy and preoccupied with the child. Where the child wishes to control and keep the mother occupied, we see the Oedipus Complex. The Oedipus Complex, as often described, is mistaken. It means different things. The meaning Socrates intended was to warn people not to put out cripples (a common practice in his time). Socrates revolted against the actions of the old Greeks. He advocated respect for all humans, strongly encouraging others to avoid cruelty, especially, cruelty toward physically disabled individuals. According to Socrates, 'If you do not trust yourself and the gods, and if you do not worship the life of each human being, you will always be in trouble.'

Looking at the construction and work of the drive, the id and the ego, we see the ego containing all the facts and actions of self-preservation. Preservation of the human race was nearly overlooked. Only one of Freud's pupils considered all of the forms of the sexual libido. This scholar said sexual libido is necessary for the welfare of the human race. On this point, considering the welfare of human race, the tenet of the sexual libido should be supported. Initially, in Freud's theory, the unconscious was thought to be filled with bad, hostile drives where everyone would like to kill everyone else. In Freud's last pamphlet, he says he 'cannot understand why he should love others.' His thinking is entirely right, if he began with the idea that the drives want to be satisfied and that suppressing these desires can be revenged. Then it is logical that he arrived at such a conclusion.

I find the descriptions offered by Freud's collaborators to be superficial notions of Freud's psychoanalysis (i.e., sadism, feelings of guilt, and so on). Making sense of Freud is hard work. I do not believe there are many persons who have really understood him. There are many persons who believe that sexuality is an important part of life. Therefore, Freudian concepts gained credibility and influence. I have never met a person who would deny the importance of sex. It always seems that if someone disagreed with a Freudian concept, it was as if this individual denied sexuality or even love. On the contrary, if it is understood that sexual urges are formed and molded from the beginning of life, then it may also be understood that the ego and the style of life guide this process.

To explain the style of life, I want to say this. It is a natural growth, continually forming, and continually molding. It represents the creative power of the individual. The individual creates understanding and meaning. Individual Psychology insists that an individual's experience is not real fact. For instance, individuals experience relationships, but they do not experience mathematical formulas. With an evolving style of life, individuals experience the ways in which they look upon things, listen, assimilate, and conclude. This is always different at the beginning of life. It happens in the realm of the 'mistake.' Psychology, like all other sciences, relies upon guessing. This is not like mathematics or logic with immediate experience. Psychology is really a hide-and-seek game with everyone looking in a different way. Individual differences cannot be explained by drives that have no direction. Freud did not explain these differences very well. The id was only one aspect. From time to time, Freud made many additions to his theory.

Regarding Freud's thoughts on the unconscious and conscious, if the unconscious is placed beyond the ego, then the ego is always attacked by the unconscious. Thus, the ego and the unconscious must be in a certain relationship and attitude. Freud believed they are in a contra-relation. Consciousness is fooled by an unformed idea. Watson would say a nonverbal idea. It is full of suppressed feelings that want to force their way through while the ego looks for self-preservation. If a person displays honesty, it is only a mask for self-preservation. It is not that the person is honest, kind, good or socially interested. There is a certain danger in this line of thinking.

Throughout the history of the human race there have been many tyrants torturing people because the tyrant believed human beings were naturally bad. Tyrants believe that people must be tamed like wild beasts. This line of thought influenced many persons. Some psychologists and educators insisted that children were like wild beasts and needed to be domesticated.

In reviewing the development of Freud's psychoanalysis, it is essential to address the Oedipus Complex. Freud suggested that boys want their mothers for their own sexual libido, and wish to kill their fathers. This line of thinking begs the question: what is the stimulus for these thoughts and actions? Individual Psychology indicates this could only occur if the child feels inferior and is striving for superiority. The child is attempting to strive from a minus to a plus. While Freud believed that children want to admire themselves and gratify themselves, Individual Psychology shows that drives are nothing more than striving from a minus to a plus.

Another incongruent idea in Freud's psychoanalysis, is Freud's notion that everyone has a death wish. Many persons facing difficulty and danger, have thought that the best solution would be death. Some individuals who are overwhelmed by difficulties would prefer to die, and some individuals attempt suicide. Striving for superiority in this way is to disappear. Persons having this death wish are pampered children.

Pampered children always want the mother for themselves alone. They do not want to join others. They exclude others, run away and look for death. They believe that if they die, it will be a terrible loss for the others. They are attempting revenge. This is an exaggerated trend of pampered children. They cannot love their neighbor, because they love only themselves. On this point the whole coherence of Freud's theory is mistaken.

One might guess that Freud was a pampered child, and his world view is that of a pampered child. In his recent book, *Civilization and Its Discontents* (Freud, 1930), he asks: Who should make this life tolerable? Should I do it alone? Everything and everyone must help. This is the cry of a pampered child. I understand why he came to this conclusion. Individual Psychology found this to be true also. But, Freud treated all neurotic persons as if they were pampered children who wanted to be pampered and appreciated. He acted as if all of his patients were always thinking of their own vanity and pride and not thinking about others. Freud has seen only such persons. He has not had broad experience, therefore, he believes this is life.

In regard to girls and women, where I have described the masculine protest as a social protest and revolt against the humiliation of girls and women, Freud used the phrase castration complex. He was afraid and terrified of being castrated or feeling that he had been castrated. These fears are an example of inferiority feelings.

Freud says people are worried and antagonistic. He infers that people fight against their unconscious, wanting it to remain unconscious. They resist revealing their unconscious. Perhaps this is why so few of Freud's pupils have understood Individual Psychology. Freud believed that all human beings are bad from nature. He also indicated that all humans were sadistic. Individual Psychology offers a different view.

We do not know how a child thinks in the prenatal stage of development. We are sure that the fate of the baby (good or bad) depends on the baby's interactions with others, especially, the mother, the father, siblings, etc. For instance, if you take a baby who is a few days old and place the baby in cold water, the baby will be inclined to cooperate with you. If however, you treat this baby rightly, and the baby is pleased with your attitude and behavior, the baby will cooperate with you. Therefore, we are right to insist that human beings are not born bad or good.

An individual's goodness is not dependent upon heredity or sexual libido. It is dependent on interactions with others. It could be mistaken in one way or another. Many persons believe it is because of the environment. Children cannot be forced to answer the influences of the environment in a mathematical way. Children answer as they want, and we cannot count on what they will answer. After we have seen that they conclude in a wrong way, we can try to help them conclude in the right way. The most important factor in bringing up children, is education.

Commentary:
Adler differentiates his views from those of Sigmund Freud by focusing on the uniqueness of the Individual. His conceptions of being and behavior are designated Individual Psychology. By this term he meant the individual was whole and undivided in specific contrast to Freud's divisions of the personality into id, ego and superego. A second contrast compares Adler's idea of goal to Freud's conception of drives. Adler gave great attention to the goal as the principal source of human movement. It is not drives that move us as Freud indicated, but where we intend to go—our fictive goal—that explains behavior. Adler was future oriented. Freud would have us believe we are subject to our drives, and we are victims of those same drives. Adler directs us to consider our creativity. He shows us that we formulate our plans, hidden or recognized, to guide movement.

An "evolving style of life" functions either to give us healthy and cooperative resolutions to the problems of living, or give us inhibiting, compensative ones that deprive us from achieving a healthy resolution. Adler found that the need for Freudian psychology to create and rely upon a succession of constructs to explain behavior only compli-

cated the process of understanding life. Adler's approach was to offer a simple solution to understand our behavior. Adler's simple approach is sometimes criticized as such, but we must also ask if Freud's complex explanations offer any improvement in understanding human behavior. Adler offers hope and optimism.

3

A Brief Comparison of Individual Psychology and Psychoanalysis

This lecture by Adler was given at the New School for Social Research in New York City. It was transcribed by Sibyl Mandell. It is too short to believe that this is the entire lecture. We presume it contains the notes on matters of contrast that Adler makes between the views of Freud and those of Individual Psychology.

The basis of Freud's theory is expressed in Individual Psychology's idea of upward striving from a feeling of inferiority to superiority. For example:

1) In order that one may not seem inferior to one's self and others, the veiling of the unconscious, Freud's so-called censor, is created and not to be separated from, the upward striving for worth and superiority.

2) The personal striving of the individual is at least as important a factor as the Oedipus Complex in the individual's relationship to father. This Freudian concept proves that the unconscious, the individual's line of thought, corresponds to the more fundamental dynamics of Individual Psychology.

3) Freud's notion of 'Narcissism' is merely another term for the well-known concept of egotism. Freud failed to acknowledge humans' interest in others and, therefore, a lack of social feeling or communal sense. Individual Psychology understands that this results from a strong feeling of inferiority. The concepts of social feeling and compensation, prescriptions for feelings of inferiority, are fundamental in Individual Psychology.

4) Freud's death wish is a misunderstood acknowledgment of weakness that occurs when an individual is confronted with reality. The death wish is not a

basic drive. Individual Psychology defines the death wish as a cowardly expression and a weak means of evasion.

5) Freud's 'ideal ego' is merely Individual Psychology's construct for social interest.

6) Freud's phrase "super ego" is an expression Individual Psychology's movement toward a fictitious goal of superiority, the striving for godlikeness.

7) The fundamental differences between Freud's psychoanalysis and Individual Psychology are not understood by psychoanalysts. According to psychoanalysts, Individual Psychology sees the striving for power as the only motivating force, which I once conceived of as a power doctrine, but later set aside as inadequate. The real differences between Freud's psychoanalysis and Individual Psychology lie in the following facts: Because of bodily limitations, it is natural for humans to express social feeling by helping each other as they face challenges. Implied in the words 'social feeling' is the notion of communal interest, the connection of persons to one another and to a sense of human solidarity. It is natural for people to be good. People only become bad, as criminals, neurotics, those considering suicide, those who are insane or perverse. For these individuals social feeling is erroneously smothered by some inner or outer influence. Then, indeed, the individual feels like a stranger in an enemy country. Not only does the individual lose interest in the well being of others, but the individual also loses contact with others. Biologically founded striving for worth is forced toward the useless side of life as the individual strives to attain a goal of personal superiority which is not in the service of others. Hence, non-social individuals (tyrants, murderers, thieves, suicidal persons or psychotic persons) differ from healthy individuals who aspire to a goal of superiority which is more on the useful side.

Commentary:
These short remarks by Adler emphasize the importance of inferiority feelings and the role they play in mental health. Freud conceived of the censor or the ego as a means for individuals to self monitor. Adler believed that individuals assess themselves relative to others. This often creates feelings of inferiority and a sense of upward striving. Adler emphasized the role of social interest relative to these feelings of inferiority. He indicates that individuals expressing social interest as they strive to overcome their feelings of inferiority will experience less psychological discomfort than those who express self interest as they strive to overcome feelings of inferiority. Everyone experiences feel-

ings of inferiority. If we are able to respond to those feelings with expressions of social interest, we will experience fewer symptoms of psychological discomfort.

4

Scientific Study of Character

This lecture was given to the Society for the Scientific Study of Character on 13 January 1930 in New York City.

In our culture one often hears the question: what is the meaning of life? What is life for? We strive in three directions: occupation, society, and intimacy. If we have a mistaken understanding of occupation, we will fail to earn a living and we will be a burden to society. Likewise, if we fail to make friends and join with society, we become isolated. If we do not develop the right attitude toward intimacy, the human race will die out.

The meaning of life is a question that each of us must address. From childhood, we create answers to this question as we grow. There are many ways to answer this question. The way in which we answer this question, influences our thoughts about self and the earth to which we are all tied.

In our culture, industriousness is a healthy answer to the question of occupation. To be lazy, would be a mistaken answer. Perhaps in another world, where industriousness was a vice, laziness would be a virtue. Living in our culture, industriousness is a virtue and the right answer to this question in life. Living on earth, humans have to work. Occupation is one of the basic connections between humans. A division of labor is important. It promotes society.

Humans are tied to their ability to connect with others. Humans do not live in isolation. Most humans have been raised in society. Individuals are responsible to one another because they live in society. It is necessary. Society solves the questions of life. Just as there are rules in games, there must be rules of conduct in society. Without rules, society would be destroyed.

Life is a challenge. There must be challenges. Humans are always questioning. A difference is seen in the life of each person, as the person answers the challenges of life. The individual may give the right answers, and get the right answers, and the individual may also make mistakes. Truth is always against those who chose the mistaken way. For instance, there once was a boy who would always pass a low door. This door opened the way to truth. If the boy wanted truth, he would have to bend himself and to use the low door. He was not forced. This boy would not bend and as a result, he had to face the consequences. We must always bear the consequences. Emerson tells us, 'Human beings always want to get rid of the consequences of their mistakes.'

If you fail to understand the meaning of life, you fail to contribute and society will say 'get away, you are useless, we don't need you.' The process of extermination has been going on since the world began. Humans can be cruel. Humans are very cruel in the persecutions of nations and races.

Some people ask what is the meaning of life, but they do not wait for an answer. They only look at it. They have already created their own meaning of life, and they are acting according to their creation. Take for instance, the child with a mistaken solution to the problems of life. The child says, 'I could solve these problems, if I were not suffering this illness.' Or the child may say, 'If I were not suffering, I would be able to solve the problems of life.' Others say, "I would like to solve the problems of life, but unfortunately I am hindered."

The meaning of life for a thief may be: 'Everything is my property.' For this individual, people and things are not private property. In the case of suicide, the meaning of life may be defined: I am bored with meeting life's problems, I don't want to solve them. I have found an easier way.

Another person who fails to meet the problems of life is the person who abuses alcohol and drugs. This person gets drunk in an effort to escape the solution to the problems of life. This person insists, 'I would have solved all the problems of life, if I had been sober.' This is an excuse. These individuals excuse themselves in this way. This is a mistaken answer. It always leads to difficulties. In later life, it is very hard to help these persons change.

Does the meaning of life originate from heredity? In some circles it is believed that whatever happens in a person's life is due to inherent abilities or disabilities. Some believe that the biological make up of an individual, the inherited traits, is so strong that the individual can do nothing on purpose. The individual might adapt a little, but not much. This way of thinking limits the individual's development. It offers an excuse and a means of avoiding the tasks of life. These individuals hide behind heredity, insisting that their problems result from inherited limits and, therefore, they exert no effort in solving the tasks of life.

People are classified by heredity. Classifying limits development. For those who believe in classifying, classifying by heredity imposes self-limits. In some negligible way, heredity seems to be a solution; this is a mistaken thought. Children who grow-up believing they have limits because of their inherited traits, do not surpass their limits, the limits given to them by others or limits they give themselves.

Since the limits of a person are unknown, it is dangerous to talk this way. Almost all humans could go farther than they do. It would be healthy to find a way to be free of these limitations. In testing these limits one should never use rules. The clinician should always attempt to understand the patient's personality, so that the clinician can see with the patient's eyes, hear with the patient's ears, and feel with the patient's heart.

The clinician should use sympathy in understanding the patient. Then the clinician can say, 'If I had the same kind of a mind and the same kind of a life as this person, I would have met the problems of life in a similar way.' Putting himself or herself in the client's place, is the best way for the clinician to truly understand and appreciate the client. In this way, the clinician can trace the origin of the meaning that the client gives to life.

Children have potentialities of meaning and potentialities of soul at the beginning of life. The first step children take in this world is to be connected with their primary care-giver, in many cases, the mother. All of the child's faculties and potentialities are tied to that connection. The child's interests are stimulated by that relationship. Skilled care-givers facilitate the healthy development of a child. The less skilled a care-giver, the less ability the child will exhibit. I do not know of any inherent potentialities, or abilities or disabilities, or favorable or unfavorable influences.

There are many interesting things to find out about a child. For instance, the time of the month in which a child is born can be of some value, but it has no great value. In a small number of cases where a child is born in winter, the child cannot go out for air, or perhaps a child is born in the hottest time of summer, when the food is good. The child begins to suffer in the beginning of life, encountering difficult circumstances by being born when it was very cold or extremely hot.

Creative striving is seen in the beginning of life. The abilities of the mind are seen in the way babies grasp things or move their fingers. Children express creativity in their environment by physical movements and certain impressions of power and ability. While the child's impressions may be mistaken, the child relies on these early impressions, all the same, to formulate meaning. The child wants to find truth. Children find truth in the experience of the body as well as experience with the environment. If there is an impression of illness or pain, the child remembers from different experiences. The meaning the child gives these experiences is probably the reason the child makes so many mistakes. Each child is different. Each of us is different. We are not all equal.

A child may have inherited disabilities, but the environment plays a greater role in the mistakes made by the child in expressing his or her scheme of life. It can be discovered which experiences are valuable in making the child's perspective more mistaken. A skilled parent can guide the child to develop in healthy ways toward healthy goals. If parents encourage a healthy point of view, the child will recognize responsibility. Healthy children are always creating, guessing, making mistakes, correcting again and again.

Some children are in a greater and more difficult position than others. They are in greater danger of developing mistaken schemes and abilities. These children are confronted more often and they are much more overburdened. It is understood that children suffering from imperfect organs, sick children, or weak children look only at their own persons. They experience difficulties and pain. They are looking for a point in the future when they will find a way to be rid of this burden. Therefore, they do not look much at the external world, but they look only at themselves.

Looking toward the future is an important point in Individual Psychology. This involves the mind of everyone because humans are moveable and wherever there is movement, there is a goal. Before movement can begin, there must be a goal. For instance, if I want to raise my arm, I could not do it, if I did not have a goal in mind. I would have no direction. This is important. Each part of my movement is involved in reaching this goal. The goal rules. The goal is the future. The future is our mind. The future is accomplishment in our mind, not the past. Both mind and bodies are in movement toward the goal.

The meaning of life is the goal in the future, a creation of the individual. In answering the question, what is the meaning of life, the solution is the goal, a goal of completion. The goal must allow the individual to feel completion, having overcome all difficulties of life, to feel superior, to be a conqueror. This is a remarkable help to the individual.

The individual goes forward striving toward a goal of superiority and arouses emotions in anticipation of the future goal. Emotions are dependent on the goal. The goal of the future is seen in movement and in the direction of the movement. It is seen in the emotions and in the actions of the movement each impression stimulates the movement.

Sometimes potentialities can be changed. If an individual suppresses symptoms, the individual has done nothing. When an adult punishes, criticizes or scolds a child because the child has misbehaved, the adult has done nothing for the child. In this situation, the adult has not changed the child's goal. If the child's goal is a mistaken meaning of life and the adult addresses only the movement, it almost always works-out that the adult has only diverted the movement. The adult must find out the mistaken goal which prompts the misbehavior.

A psychiatrist once said, 'You can understand a person if you don't assume him to be a unit.' I would contribute more to this assumption. I would say that nothing is created because of the goal. If all of the movements of the mind are running toward this goal, in which the person feels useful and completes the questions of life, then this goal is a unity. It is important to understand this unity of the individual, the individual's personality, characteristics, thoughts, feelings, actions and so on. It seems reasonable to come to the following conclusion: to understand rightly the parts, the impressions, the movements, the characteristics, feelings and behaviors, one must understand the unity of the person. All of these experiences work in relation to the individual's expression of social interest. Personality is built-up relative to the individual's goal of superiority. It is like a melody of the individual having sounds and vibrations. When the sounds and vibrations are understood, the meaning is clear.

To understand the child, it is wise to look at a situation in which the child does not feel strong enough to compete. This is a situation where the child feels inferior to others. Feelings of inferiority are common. The inferiority complex is more of an illness than inferiority. The feeling of inferiority can be worthwhile if it stimulates the individual toward a socially useful goal of superiority which improves society in some way.

This feeling of inferiority is never tested as a disease. The attitude is classified in this way: a person may experience feelings of inferiority on the one side, and in another situation the same individual feels worthwhile. This means that one must be worthwhile with regard to all persons. As long as this feeling is known and not trained, it does not work. It takes more than training. In the beginning of life, the primary care-giver teaches the child to be interested in the well-being of others. Many speak of education. Good education means that children learn to be interested in the well-being of others.

In many homes, the primary care-giver is the mother. The greatest part of cultural life (work and progress in social causes), is due to mothers. Mothers accomplish the greatest work in the world, which is for the welfare of the human race. While this work is not paid for, it should never be undervalued.

Fathers also have responsibility for helping children find their goals of superiority and usefulness while contributing cooperatively to the welfare of the larger society. It is possible for both parents to make mistakes. For instance if the parents foster the children's interest in the parents, but not the larger social group, this is a mistake. You will find many pampered children lacking interest in others.

Children who are suffering from imperfect organs, long term illness, neurosis, dementia praecox and so on will also express a lack of interest in others. These children are in danger of forming egotistical interests. They may feel they are not able to contribute, and that they are not worthwhile. They are deprived. They cannot express interest in others. They tend to be focused on their own difficulties.

Neglected children found in orphanages, illegitimate children, unwanted children, children with disabilities, and those living in institutions, are deprived of role models who might teach the children to be interested in the welfare of others. No one has expressed an interest in them. Therefore, they do not know there is such a thing as social interest. It is very difficult to interest these children in the welfare of others. Often, they develop egotistical characteristics. They are overburdened and very reserved. They look to their own welfare, no further. They have no friends. They are problem children. These are not feeble-minded children. Feeble-minded children lack the right instruments for development.

Children with a low degree of intelligence cannot be compared to problem children of average or above average intelligence. However, it is possible to compare the two expressions. One child is egotistical and the other is cooperative. They conclude differently. If a person is hurt, the egotistical child will laugh. The other child will run to help the injured person. They look at what is happening in different ways. The whole style of life of the egotistical child is mistaken. The child who laughs when another is hurt, laughs not only in a bad manner, but also in a hateful manner.

Individual Psychology offers guidelines for what must be done. By understanding an individual's life style, the clinician will understand the individual's mistaken meaning of life. When the individual's perspective is understood, it is possible to guide the client toward change. Inferiority feelings arise when a child is discouraged by believing that he or she is not strong enough or able enough to address the challenges at hand. The child may be ashamed, always jumping from one situation to another. What are children to do when confronted with difficulties? If these children do not receive encouragement, they will not improve. Children must be taught a better awareness of themselves. Children must be encouraged.

Discouraged children are a problem in the family, in school and in society. Adults discourage too much. Adults punish and insist on changing children's mistaken view, instead of increasing children's ability to cooperate. By punishing and criticizing, adults decrease children's spirit of cooperation, their abilities and potentialities.

Courage is the ability to cooperate and to express social interest. Only individuals who feel that they are part of the whole, who feel as if they are at home on the earth, who expect both advantages and disadvantages, who sense a feeling of belonging when with others, are the individuals who express courage. Courage is seen only on the useful side of life, in solving the problems of work, society, and intimacy. The useless side of life does not insist on courage.

Children who express a mistaken meaning of life, perhaps on the egotistical side, want to boss others. These children do not express courage. They are only aggressive toward others when the responses and limits of the others are known. If a dangerous dog barks at these children, the children do not argue any more. They undervalue others. They will become argumentative and aggressive which are behaviors on the useless side. Also, on the useless side, children may resort to using force to get their own way. They like to hinder others in their escape from the problems of life.

Courage is not seen among criminals. They resist the problems of occupation. With a gun in hand, they believe they are courageously accomplishing what they want, which is on the useless side of life. When the thief deprives others by using the arguments of the gun or by using the dark, the thief is not courageous. It is not courageous to conquer others.

People who act on the useless side of life, toward goals of personal superiority, may believe they are more clever than the police. Their pride is centered on being more clever than the police. Their whole meaning in life is to be superior to the police. This does not agree with common sense. It is a sort of personal superiority. This might be the sort of pride that is seen in many nations who do not act cooperatively, who do not share intelligence and so they conclude differently. The mistaken scheme is that these individuals are looking out only for themselves, their own personal needs, and their own personal interests. This is not common sense.

Understanding has a common meaning. Humans can understand in a private manner. As they understand, they expect others to understand. That is the meaning they give to life. Interest in others involves all of the individual's faculties, all of the individual's abilities, all of the individual's possibilities, reasoning, looking, speaking, and understanding. The faculties of common sense play the highest role in the development of cooperation. Therefore, Individual Psychology, insists beyond this phase, beyond these limits, it looks at an individual's striving for superiority and the individual's degree of cooperation. The language of such limits does not exist in Individual Psychology.

In science, whatever stimulates or depresses a person, will stimulate and depress another person in the same way. This is for the psychiatrists. It is not psychology. It is not what we mean if we want to understand a person, for instance, insisting if you depress one side of a certain desire it jumps to the other side. This is also the mechanical construction of psychiatrists, but in Individual Psychology it does not exist. It is biology and cannot be counted upon.

When an individual strives toward the useful side of life, the individual feels worthwhile. Accompanying this feeling is a sense of happiness. Happiness always depends upon the individual's degree of cooperation. Where there is happiness, there will also be a sense of accomplishment. Individuals feel useful when they accomplish worthwhile things. This creates feelings of happiness. To feel worthwhile, the individual must strive in the line of cooperation and social interest.

Commentary:
Creative striving is a theme in this lecture. How an individual addresses the meaning of life relates to the individual's creative striving and fictive goals. Signs of this creativity are seen in the activity of young children as they explore and seek to know. Skilled parents foster this process. Less skilled parents may discourage the child. Parents can thwart the child's natural movement toward mastery. They may do this from two different perspectives. They may purposefully neglect the child and prevent development, or they may pamper the child and inhibit self-development and personal competency. The former causes delay in natural development. It is easily identified. The latter is more subtle because it appears as parental concern when, in fact, it keeps the child from developing independence. Both approaches impede the child's movement toward self-mastery.

Adler advises against classifying and labeling individuals. Classification imposes limits. Individuals are capable of many things. Adler encourages us to think of in terms of unlimited potential. He encourages us to reach beyond our self imposed limits and encourages us to meet life's challenges with courage and cooperation so that we express social interest in all that we do.

5

Courage

This lecture was transcribed by Bernard S. Knauer. The exact date and occasion are not known. Teaching Courage is directed toward parents and teachers encouraging them to foster courage in students. Adler specifies a cooperative relationship between teachers and students which means that teachers must recognize students as equal participants in the education process.

In this speech, Adler provides specific ideas about how to implement the teaching of courage. Note Adler's mention of the "life-lie." Adler wrote a paper entitled "Life-Lie and Responsibility" in 1914. A life-lie is created or constructed in order to placate and sooth the self-esteem injured by feelings of inferiority. The Norwegian playwright, Henrik Ibsen invented this neologism which received mention in his play, The Wild Duck, published in 1884. Adler appropriated this term. It is also interesting to note that "life-history" replaces "life-lie," but presages "Life Style." Adler used a great variety of terms for elucidating this concept. (See Adler, A. 1914; Stone, 1997a, Stone, 1997b; and Stone, 2002, for further discussion of the Life-Lie).

If anyone wished to make sure that children grow up to be failures in life, the method would be perfectly simple. There are only two things to do—systematically discourage children, and keep them isolated from other children.

The techniques of discouragement are many. Punish children, and they will learn that you are strong and they are very weak. They will not give up trying to show their importance, but will feel bound to fail. If they ask questions, tell them, "You will understand when you are older." This will again show them that you do not regard them as equals. They will stop asking questions and become stupid. Always appear anxious about their health, and excessively warn them about the dangers of going out alone, or about doing anything for themselves. They will then believe that life is much too difficult. They will hesitate and become timid, and will always be looking for an easy way out. They will not cease to struggle; for all humans struggle as long as they are alive. However, they will struggle in useless ways, and they will struggle without courage.

Isolate children from other children, and they will never learn how to fit in with other people. They will go through life without knowing that friendship and cooperation are possible. They will never feel at home in society. When they are confronted with the problems of adult life, they will be helpless. All problems are social problems; involving other people as well as ourselves.

These problems can only be solved if we are interested in others. There is no exception to this rule. It we have not been trained to help others and be helped by them, we will not learn ways to meet life with success. Consider for example the problem of marriage: Is it possible that anyone should succeed in marriage if they have not learned to cooperate? Is it possible that they can succeed in marriage if they have not learned to be interested in others?

It is important to realize that, although social feeling may be inborn in every one of us, it still needs to be trained and developed. At every point in the training of a child, the development of social feeling may be blocked; the child may be turned away from interest in the larger world. Every failure can be attributed to a block in the development of social feeling. None of us want our children to be failures. We can see plenty of evidence that discouraged individuals become badly equipped for life without making the experiment of deliberate discouragement.

Let us draw out from these considerations some positive guidance for the training of responsible, useful and successful human beings. First, perhaps, we should define a little closer what we mean by courage. Real courage is always useful courage, and it is always courageous to meet the common problems of life. It is not the same thing as heroism; though heroism itself is, perhaps, no more than the application of common courage in unusual difficulties.

What I wish to make clear is this: We should not call persons courageous who are always seeking tests of courage and to see how much they can stand. It is plain that such persons are trying to prove themselves heroes because they are afraid that they are cowards. We always find in them a lack of confidence, and we could suspect that they are avoiding the real problems and difficulties in the situation. Many people make up these fictitious tests of strength—how much pain can I bear? Should I be frightened? If I were in great danger, can I establish an endurance record? All of them are trying to conceal cowardice.

If a person went through life with unlimited courage, that person would never evade the problems of occupation of friendship, or of love. This individual might make mistakes, of course, for we learn by our mistakes; but these mistakes would be small, and this individual would never make the same mistake twice. One of the highest expressions of courage is the courage to be imperfect, the courage to risk failure and to be proved wrong. This individual would be a good worker, since the person would have been trained to do things for himself or herself. By practice this individual would gain the skill to do the right thing at the right time, and would have a succession of real achievements. This person would work with a goal, and what was started would be completed. This individual would be a good friend, not afraid of offending others, but always interested in the welfare of others. Self-initiated, this individual would contribute to the lives of others by useful and fitting means. We would not see this individual waiting for the approval of others. Nor would we see this person acting reserved, hesitant or introverted. That would be plain cowardice. This individual would be a true partner in love, and there would be no need to exaggerate self worth at the expense of someone else. This person would not fear the loss of love and would have learned that the only way to secure love is to enrich and ease the life of another person.

Defeat and difficulty would be only a stimulus to increase efforts and skill. This individual would never display self pity or make claims for special consideration. This person would be occupied, not with self, but with the tasks of life. The only reason for an individual to be self occupied is the fear of defeat. If introverts were sure of success, they would be changed in a minute.

Courageous individuals are engaged at all points of human life: They do not suffer a threat by saying 'this is beyond me.' In all of their problems they would be reckoning, as far as they are able, with the whole situation. No doubt, if they were called on to deal with unusual circumstances, they would meet them with unusual courage: But it would really be the same courage that they had trained themselves to apply to ordinary circumstances and ordinary decisions.

In our actual life we do not find anyone who has kept courage undiminished. To a greater or lesser degree, we have all set limits to ourselves and have excused ourselves from making full use of our efforts. The degree of our courage, however, and the consequent degree of our ability to cooperate, is the index of our psychic health. The true way to solve any problem is always to apply more courage and more cooperation. Any failure in courage can only make the situation more difficult. Most important of all, we have found, using the techniques of Individual Psychology, the way to encourage those who shrink before the difficulties of life, and to develop and train the courage of children so that they are not soured by the reverses experienced early in life.

It would be a great advantage for the future of the human race if our teachers and educators could come to an agreement in their aims. At present, the development of the child is left too much to private theories and prejudices. Before the goal of education is fixed, it would be a profitable task to pass under review all the standpoints of any promise. Already, however, we might come to an agreement on a few points, because they are incontestable or, at least, because they are in harmony with common sense and have a prescriptive place in the goal of education. It seems to me that, in our own day, three demands are the most worthy of attention. First, the ideal in education must be applicable to everybody. Second, it must be clear and intelligible. Third, it must assure usefulness to the community.

Let me take these conditions one by one. The ideal in education must be applicable to everybody. To everybody, I mean, all who are capable of receiving any education. We often exclude those who seem impaired, due to our present state of knowledge, and are thought to be mental cripples. We must eliminate everything that separates children, as if the one part of them were to be made into masters, and the other into slaves. We must also prefer methods to facilitate progress for all children, even to those who seem less gifted. We should not consider it of first importance to discover concealed talents, nor should we overestimate obvious abilities. Our aim should be to awaken the capacities of all children.

In our current day the possibility of developing, in every child, mental, physical and moral abilities, is still too low. No one can succeed in extending these limits unless freed from the superstition that these capacities are fixed and constant. Therefore, educators should select those methods which are best adapted to encourage the efforts of pupils and increase their courage, rather than restrict them and keep them within special boundaries.

The ideal must be clear and intelligible. We cannot decide by consulting our own feelings or the force of tradition. Agreement can come only through understanding. The true ideal will show itself in the independence and self-confidence of teachers and pupils in their work. They must be able to fit the aim of education into the knowledge they have gained from their own experiences. I recommend the findings of Individual Psychology as the best guide for understanding their tasks. Individual Psychology sees a human life as a creative effort, the end being to make approximately right solutions to the three problems of life—the relation to occupation, to society and to the other sex. From the fact that it is a creative effort, it follows that only the courageous individuals can devote themselves wholeheartedly to the tasks of life. It must assure usefulness to the community.

Every action outside the framework of use to the community can only diminish the individual's worthwhile feeling, and hence restrict the individual's confidence and courage. Useless actions give individuals a feeling of inferiority. These feelings put us in conflict with others. New difficulties follow automatically whenever the logic of our life in association with others is violated. If an individual's actions are useless, the individual feels that others are hostile. The only way this person can secure a feeling of importance and significance is by all sorts of lies, excuses, strategies and self-justifications. These behaviors only make life harder. As long as children trust themselves to gain importance on the useful side of life, they will retain and develop courage.

For Individual Psychology the recognition of the truth, 'I can be courageous only if I feel worthwhile and I can feel worthwhile only if my actions are useful to the community,' is the first step in the awakening of courage. These statements form a unity. They serve as the basis for discussions about the aims of education. Each one of them sows the central necessity for training in courage. If additional evidence is necessary, I need only point to the results of a mistaken education most troublesome to the educator. These are the problem children, the neurotics (who are well-called "nervous"), drunkards, individuals contemplating suicide, criminals and prostitutes. All these people have lost their courage to succeed on the useful side of life. It will be easily understood that they have all felt—rightly or wrongly—that they were excluded from the ideal of education, but our educational methods were not applicable to them. In every case we could show this from their life-history. They can only be won back if they gain the courage to claim significance on the side of common sense and the feeling of fellowship, not in opposition to it.

Now, let me recall some of the practical ways in which parents and teachers may help to build up and develop courage in their children. First of all, they must never regard their own greater strength, or wider experience as enabling them to dictate to children. If children obey because they are forced to obey, their courage is already broken. Parents and teachers should regard children as their equals, and regard their own knowledge, not as proving personal superiority, but as showing that they have had a longer time to learn. The more this consciousness of real human equality is shown, and the less parents and teachers behave as infallible authorities, the more likely the children entrusted to them grow up and become courageous and independent adults.

Here is the second point. From the very first day of life, children should be trained to be as independent as their age allows. The more things that children can do for themselves, the greater will be their self-confidence and ability to adapt. There is nothing more discouraging for children than to feel that they must always be helped—that they are not able to do their work by themselves or play their games by themselves. Of course, if adults are always over-anxious for their children, they will teach children to expect that the world is a very dangerous place, and that to be alive is a very great hardship.

Anxiety is never useful; real dangers and difficulties can be faced better if we are levelheaded.

The "only child" is particularly liable to suffer from the anxious parents. Often this is because the parents place all their ambitions and hopes on the shoulders of an only child. They overburden the child with expectations, they wish to guard and oppress the child, and they cannot bear to let the child take any risks. Sometimes an additional reason is present—the parents decided to have only one child because they were afraid of the economic difficulties of having more than one. They were already pessimistic and cowardly in their view of life and their interpretation of their own capacities. They showed a similar cowardice in considering the fate of this child.

It is always best for child to have the society of children of his or her own age and attainments; for with this group, the child can best learn companionship and cooperation. Here, children compare themselves with those who are of the same age, similar ability and experience. Moreover, it is only in society that courage can be trained.

No one ever succeeds in becoming courageous by thinking about courage, or by separating from the group and determining to be courageous. Courage can only be learned in practice. The foundation for all courage is social courage—courage in our relationships with others.

Finally, it should be said that courage and cooperation can only be learned from those who are themselves courageous and cooperative. The individual who faces the problems of life without seeking an easy way out, who feels at home with the human race, and who acts well-equipped to continue the creative effort of living, is best in training others to express courage. Courage is as contagious as cowardice. It we have kept our courage, we can help others in developing their own.

Commentary:

In this lecture Adler demonstrates the influence of courage on human development. Developing the courage required to meet life's challenges is a life-long process. It springs from modest attempts as a young child to greater and greater expression in later years. When the encouragement process is lacking, children are hesitant of meeting challenges for fear of failure and other imagined outcomes. Carried to extremes, a lack of courage keeps an adult from achieving any goals, because it thwarts even the beginning steps necessary for any progress to take place.

Parenting means encouraging the child in the adventure of learning and doing. Increasing the amount of self-directed exploration allows the child to grow in self-mastery. Not allowing the child these opportunities inadvertently conveys to the child a message that growing up is dangerous. Such an approach to child-rearing keeps a normal approach to growth and mastery from occurring. Adult manifestations from this false practice cause persons to doubt their ability to handle challenges and prevents them from fully enjoying life.

6

Bashfulness

In this lecture Adler describes bashfulness, examines the etiology of bashfulness and offers suggestions for treating bashfulness. This lecture was transcribed by Alan Porter. The date and occasion of this lecture are unknown.

Bashfulness is one of the most disagreeable feelings and at the same time one of the most common. Sometimes it is severest in childhood, and as children grow up they become more confident. Everyone has seen the shy child, shrinking from strangers, unwilling to speak or answer questions, or hiding in mothers' arms or behind her back. If this child is treated in a friendly way, the bashfulness will diminish. Often, however, bashfulness increases with adolescence. Many adolescents become adults who are always awkward and ill at ease amongst their peers.

When individuals are bashful, they show it in all their expressions. They cannot speak freely, their look is embarrassed, and even their thoughts are impeded. Sometimes they feel as if they were paralyzed, or they begin to tremble and perspire. A blush may appear on the face. They may have difficulty in breathing and feel that they are choking. Perhaps they make senseless movements with their hands. Often in a fit of bashfulness, an individual begins to swallow air, and in consequence, the stomach and digestive system may occasionally be affected.

Here, we can see how bashful individuals feel and how their feelings are expressed in external appearances. The person who suffers from bashfulness can tell us something of the process, and we ourselves can observe some of the results. If we are to understand bashfulness, there are several important questions to which we must find an answer. First of all, what is the meaning of bashfulness? Next, when a bashful person is free from symptoms and outward signs is this person still bashful, or does this person behave bashfully in certain situations? If the second is true, what are the characteristics of these situations? Finally, can bashfulness be cured and if so how?

Bashful people behave as if they were in a dangerous or at least painful situation. Their mind is under great tension on occasions, which, to the majority of us, would not seem of any importance. These individuals suffer. Tension flares-up whenever a bashful person has to approach someone outside the close circle of family and friends (for example, if a bashful person enters a shop, or goes into company, or meets other people, especially those who are considered above in status.)

These individuals have certain recognition of the existence of other people. They are not trying to avoid them entirely, but they show, rather, an unusual caution, a hesitating attitude in approaching others. Bashful individuals are playing opossum. They are waiting to see how the other person will behave. Their recognition of others is always combined with a feeling of dependence on others, a fear of their opinion, and a strange expectation of hostility. Bashful individuals wish to come nearer, but they are afraid of being rebuffed. In consequence, their relation with others can never be natural and unaffected. They can never be spontaneous. There is a very strong resemblance between bashfulness and stage fright.

So far, it is not particularly easy to understand why a bashful individual does not believe that relations with others can be mutually harmless and pleasant. We are driven to suppose that these individuals have a strange feeling that other people will not be good-natured; will not be up to the bashful person's standard. Perhaps other people will be difficult to handle or other people will turn out to be enemies. Perhaps other people will despise bashfulness, criticize and undervalue the bashful person. The meeting may not be a success. The stranger may not recognize the importance of the bashful person. Bashful people are always pursued by doubts and always expect to be underrated.

The Roots of Bashfulness

Individuals who are always sure of success could never be bashful. There is only one reason on earth why people hesitate, doubt, stop their progress or try to escape from the problems of life. Anyone in this position is afraid of defeat, afraid of depreciation. Therefore, in cases of bashfulness, a great tension arises, from the fear of defeat, reproach, or criticism. Why are some people especially tortured by this fear of defeat? What mental organization leads to such an attitude, to such a defective adaptation to our social life? Are they people who are really inferior, who know it, and try to keep it a secret? No one can measure the worth of another person. No one can be placed in the position of judge. It is impossible to regard one human being as inferior to another.

Suppose I really were inferior—is that the end of the story? Am I entirely powerless? Are there no means of improvement? Must I remain in the future what I have been in the past? I can improve if I find the right method in education, in culture, in social standard, in appearance, and in all the activities of life. Only a low opinion of my own possibilities will keep me back.

We must agree, of course, that the bashful individual is not very optimistic, not very hopeful. The bashful person's courage and self-confidence are low. These persons do not expect much of themselves, but are unaware of it. Perhaps you prove to them in the most pleasant and friendliest possible manner that they have a poor opinion of themselves. They will still deny it. But in their behavior the fact appears very plainly. If we shut our ears to their words and observe their actions, we shall see that they do not trust themselves.

Bashful people over rate others making them into judges and so become dependent on their verdict. Even before they have approached a fellow being, they are dependent on what they expect the opinion to be. Even before words are spoken, they are afraid that the other person will disagree. And, of course, feeling insecure with themselves, they want to avoid being judged. They try to escape decisions about their own worth and value. All the time they are consumed with the idea "Don't get any closer, don't get found out. Put off the test. Escape the verdict." It is this style of life, which accounts for all their hesitation in speech and manner.

Here we see the chief difference between bashful people and those whose attitude is more normal. When persons have courage and self-confidence, and find themselves in difficulties, they do what can be done to alter and improve the situation. They go on striving. Difficulties are merely a stimulus to further effort. But bashful individuals are suffering from heightened feelings of inferiority, and from their supposed inferiority. They draw the conclusion, 'You can't do any better. You are bound to fail. You must stop trying.' Instead of being courageous and going ahead they block their own activities and concentrate on avoiding depreciation.

Why are they so dependent on the opinion of others? Why do they need appreciation so much? It is because they are so self-centered. The goal of all bashful people is to be appreciated without contributing to the happiness of others in social intercourse. Bashful people wish that others should confess their worth whether or not they do useful actions. They want to be popular without being agreeable. It is an impossible demand to fulfill, and we need not wonder that they suffer from such a tension.

We shall generally find behind bashful individuals a childhood in which they were pampered by their parents or by other members of the environment. These children were trained to expect appreciation just because they happened to be alive. They did not see that they could win appreciation by their own independent activities, by making the lives of others happier and more fruitful. It was in these circumstances that they arrived at a low opinion of their own possibilities, their fear of defeat, and their fear of hostile judgments from people outside the circle of those who pampered them.

The trouble with bashful individuals is the same as with everyone else whose attitude is mistaken. They cannot forget themselves. Instead of being interested in the life around them and in their fellow human beings, they are always attending to their own feelings, wondering whether they are giving a good enough account of themselves, asking, 'What do they think of me? Am I appreciated properly? Are they giving me enough consideration?' Persons who are always wondering whether they are getting enough from others can never be satisfied.

People who insist most on their own dignity and importance are the very people who are most easily hurt. If someone they know passes them in the street without noticing them, they feel humiliated and insulted. It is the same with bashful people. An instance of carelessness or lack of attention, which anyone else would overlook, plunges the bashful person into the deepest inferiority feeling. Bashful people are always looking for such instances. They are compelled to decrease their interest in real tasks and real achievements. People are not bashful when they are occupied with work or when they are interested in the people and things around them. In consequence, bashful people diminish their sphere of activity and lose many opportunities of happiness and success.

One of the most important demands of our social life is that we should be able to forget about ourselves and consider others. We must be able to see with the eyes of others, listen with their ears, and feel with their hearts. We must be able to devote our whole power to the tasks we undertake without being distracted by questions of our own importance. We must be looking for opportunities to give and to contribute, not merely to receive and to be recognized. Our attitude must be like that of a good hostess, who is happy in so far as her guests are in a good humor.

Bashful persons must learn to forget themselves and bear other people in mind. If they were interested in others, there would be no sense in bashfulness. It would disappear immediately. It is their goal of being appreciated without contributing that keeps them bashful and involves them in suffering.

The cure should begin at the earliest stages of bashfulness. Bashful people should be understood in all the ramifications of their desire to be pampered. Their bashfulness is merely a claim that we should handle them with our gloves on, that we should all be especially careful and tender with them; we must show them all the ways in which they are demanding special consideration. We must reveal their pessimistic attitude with regard to their own careers. We must point out how they cling to people with whom they are familiar, to their own family and especially, perhaps to their mothers. They must be acquainted with all the examples of their attitude that we can collect. They must be convinced of their meaning.

Such a treatment must be carried through in a tactful and comradely manner. The individual must see from our own attitude that they have nothing to fear from the criticism of their fellows. In the end, they will be able to see that failure is the result of a mistaken opinion of their own capacities and of the mistaken importance they have given to the opinion of others. It is obvious that bashfulness is closely connected with stammering, blushing and self-consciousness, and with neurosis and psychosis in general. All of them result from a preoccupation with one's own feelings and low degree of interest in people, work, and things. The beginnings of bashfulness in childhood should, therefore, be carefully watched and corrected. We can always accomplish this by winning the child's cooperation and interesting him in others.

Commentary:

Adler reminds us that bashful persons tend to be overly cautious and slow to trust others. Their feelings of distrust stem from mistaken childhood perceptions. They end up believing it is less uncomfortable to express shyness than to take risks. Bashfulness offers an excuse from participation. By such behavior, bashful persons excuse themselves from activities. Continually practicing this avoidance only increases the problem.

Frequently, the bashful person harbors dreams of success. But hesitation gets in the way and dreams of accomplishment supplant actual progress. By hesitating one avoids imagined failure and embarrassment, but by hesitating one also misses opportunities.

7

Finicky Eating

This lecture was given at the Long Island College of Medicine, Brooklyn, New York on 21 December 1932. Adler focuses on the difficulties many parents face at dinnertime. He touches on the topics bulimia and anorexia.

Finicky eating is one of the most wide spread problems of childhood that confronts physicians, pediatricians and parents. In such cases we must first exclude possible illnesses as the cause. Frequent illness after birth can cause a spasm of the pylorus. This was not known for a long time. I believe the first operation was performed fifteen years ago in Berlin under the advice of Finckelstein. Since that time more and more cases have been found.

Finicky eating is really a matter of diagnosis. What I usually find among children who do not want to eat or children who vomit is that these children are pampered. This fact must be investigated. You will find that pampered children are the centers of attention within the family. Their parents tend to be especially frightened by the symptoms, much more than is necessary. No child with this symptom has ever starved, but of course, finicky eating does not benefit the development of a young child. It can start very early in the child's life. You may see it when the child is two, three, four months of age. In regard to such cases, we must remember that babies have different taste than grown-ups.

Perhaps you have heard of the experiments conducted in Chicago by a pediatrician who let children around the age of two have their own choice in the food they would eat. The pediatrician offered the children eggs, bread, butter, salt, sugar, coffee tea, etc. and let the children choose whatever they wanted to eat. As a result, the children developed very well even though they sometimes ate things which might frighten physicians. For instance a child would eat five eggs at one time and as a result did very well. We must remember that children have different tastes.

Today some remedies have been made from cod liver oil. Children with rickets are very fond of cod liver oil. Other children resent it. It as though nature provides taste for our needs and we have instincts in regard to eating which we do not use or we lose after some time.

I am sure that drunkards have a different taste than others. Drunkards have a different taste in regard to liquor than the average person. They feel more in drinking. When I am with people who like to drink, I have often seen how fond they are of liquor. They beam in anticipation and in the enjoyment of drinking. Others cannot understand drinking.

If a pampered child resists taking certain food and the child finds that the parents are paying more attention, the child begins to control the parents. This reinforces the child's resistance to eating the foods. Babies and young children vomit easily. They learn the art of vomiting. In response parents may express anxiety over the child and resort to tricking the child into eating. Sometimes the parents use storytelling as a means of reasoning with the child. Sometimes they make promises. Sometimes tricks are successful, but in more serious cases, they are of no use. We must think of other ways. There is no rule that one way or another is always successful. Sometimes success is attained if the parents are not present when the child is eating. Sometimes it is helpful for the child to be placed in the society of other children at mealtime. Sometimes it helps to take the food away if the child does not eat. This may help if the symptom of finicky eating has not lasted a long time.

Children may combine this symptom with other problems, school, for instance. They do not want to eat breakfast before going to school. You will always see how adults are afraid in such cases and make a great fuss over the child. This, of course is what the child likes. Thus, the child will continue the habit.

There are more strategies that can be used. Perhaps the best I have seen is to have another person, perhaps children at the table. They will sit quietly for awhile. After some time one may ask 'what is wrong with our food today? Perhaps the cook has forgotten.' Then everyone must wait quietly. The children will start to counteract this waiting. The adults must be patient. Everyone must wait. After awhile, when the children become expectant, the food arrives and the children eat.

Sometimes these strategies work and sometimes they do not. It is necessary to encourage the child to be as independent as possible. It is important to refrain from pampering the child. It is always great trouble for children when their parents overemphasize anything, whether it is bowel movements, bathing or masturbation. Children find it convenient to utilize their parent's concerns as a means of controlling the parents.

Later in life you may also find resistance against eating. I have described this symptom as a hunger strike. I have found it only among young women. I once saw a young woman, eighteen years of age who weighed sixty pounds. She moved about like a skeleton so that others took pity on her. It appears that this hunger strike always appears when the pampered individual experiences a great disappointment and believes this disappointment is impossible to overcome. In such a case it is necessary to change the whole style of life. It is also necessary to change the style of life of the child who acts finicky about eating. It is most important to help these individuals become more cooperative. They must feel as if they are a part of the whole. We must be very careful in such cases. We must consider stomach trouble in an organic way and exclude it before we proceed. We must also be able to exclude other illnesses.

It is not difficult to understand that a feverish child suffering from an infectious illness will not have an appetite. Sometime organic illness is not seen in the right way. Sometimes children become peevish and do not wish to eat. I have seen children who stopped eating after they had eaten very well. When you know that a child behaves independently and not pampered, then you must be suspicious. There are real reasons why children do not want to eat. We must be careful. Sometimes when a child refuses to eat, the refusal may be a symptom of tubercular meningitis. Differential diagnosis is always important. We must look at all sides. We must not overlook anything which might explain the symptom. In cases where an organic reason is not involved, we can be sure the child has been pampered and wishes to control others by refusing to eat. The individual does not wish to cooperate. The individual strives to overcome problems in a mistaken way. The goal of the finicky individual is to control others. Therefore, it is important for us to encourage this individual to cooperate and to increase expressions of social interest.

Commentary:

Adler makes a simple diagnostic test for discerning the difference between physical manifestations and psychological ones. Adler reminds us that there is a physical basis for some of the symptoms related to eating problems and that pampered children are manifesting lifestyle convictions. This difference often applies to many human complaints. Adler's remarks are geared toward differentiating individuals with health concerns and individuals intent on non-cooperative behaviors.

For some individuals who are striving for perfection, finicky eating leads to anorexia or bulimia. If this is the case, we must encourage these individuals to meet life *with courage and help them accept imperfections. In some instances finicky eating occurs when an individual appraises a situation and believes another is over-controlling. As we consider issues related to anorexia and bulimia, we are wise to consider an individual's perceptions of perfection, independence and control.*

8

Laziness

The lecture was transcribed by Alan Porter. The date, occasion and transcription of this lecture are unknown. Adler offers an understanding of laziness and offers suggestions for encouraging industriousness.

What are the motives of the lazy child? First we will exclude children with organic deficiencies, children who suffer from anaemia, tuberculosis, those who have difficulty breathing through the adenoids or nose obstructions, deficiencies of the thyroid gland, and other such conditions. We will also exclude those children whose laziness is a direct attack on their parents and teachers. Laziness can sometimes be an act of revenge. It is a very good weapon for disappointing others and causing trouble.

In all other cases of laziness we look for a fear of defeat in work, games, or school activities. A fear of defeat always brings about a lack of interest. When children think that they can solve a problem, they take an interest in it. Interest in a subject is the strongest stimulus to master it. If children are interested, they enjoy learning. But, when children are afraid that they cannot succeed, they gradually distract their interest from the subject.

Success is a word that is understood differently by everyone. Sometimes it is astonishing to find out what a child regards as a defeat. There are many individuals who think they are defeated if they are not ahead of all the others. Even if they are successful, they consider it a defeat if someone does better.

How does striving for superiority and completeness show itself in laziness? Lazy individuals never experience defeat because they never face the test. They exclude the problem before them. They postpone the decision about whether or not they can compete with others. Moreover, everyone else is more or less sure that if lazy individuals were less lazy, they could meet with difficulties. Lazy individuals take refuge in the satisfying thought, 'if only I were not lazy, then I could do everything.' Whenever lazy individuals fail, they diminish the fact of the failure and keep their self esteem, saying 'It is only laziness, and not a lack of ability.'

Sometimes teachers say to a lazy student, 'If you would work harder, you could be the most brilliant student in the room.' Why should lazy individuals work? They can keep their reputation without working. Maybe if the lazy individual were to stop acting lazy, the reputation for concealed brilliance would come to an end. The individual would be judged on real accomplishments, not on what might have been.

There is another personal advantage in acting lazy. If this individual does the least bit of work, there is praise for the effort. From a more industrious person, this small effort would not have been noticed. When a teacher asked a lazy child why he was not working, the child replied "I know I'm the laziest boy in the class, but you are always paying attention to me. The boy next to me is the best student in the class, but you never notice him.'

Lazy individuals consider their own interest. They are not trying to contribute. They are looking for the easiest way in life. They occupy the time and attention of others and they expect others to support and help them. In all of this we can see the egotistical attitude of the lazy individual. We can hardly blame the lazy person however. Healthy children are not naturally lazy. They become lazy artificially. They have been pampered by their parents. From infancy these children have trained themselves to expect everything from the efforts of others.

Commentary:

Adler asks, "What is the goal of laziness?" If we understand the individual's goal, we will gain an understanding of the individual's behavior. Behavior serves the goal. It is explained by one's goal(s) and not by causes.

Like the individual who is expressing bashfulness, the individual who is expressing laziness, avoids meeting life's challenges. When presented with situations that create feelings of inferiority, the individual saves face by presenting with laziness. These individuals have become discouraged about contributing to society. Rather than risk disappointment, they avoid the tasks at hand.

9

Mistakes of Childhood

The date, occasion and transcription of this lecture are unknown. Adler offers an understanding of children's motivation. He also addresses mistaken attitudes and behaviors while explaining the principles of Individual Psychology.

Children's mental and social growth never proceed in a straight line. No living creature grows without some variation from the ideal without making some detour and falling short in one way or another from the best we might expect. It is the task of education to find out these variations, detours, and shortcomings as they begin. We must recognize the child's motives and see them as part of the child's whole development. Then, we must discover how to correct these mistakes.

All the mistakes made by children fall into one pattern. They are mistakes due to the child's attitude and the child's expectations of life. In consequence, it will never help the child, if we concentrate on one mistake only and try to correct this single mistake. We must inquire, watch, and listen until we can understand the child's whole approach to life.

Another task of education is to avoid exposing children to those influences, impressions and experiences which we know, by our own experience, by logic and common sense, hamper their development. This does not mean that we should forbid children certain activities. Prohibitions either make children cowards or stimulate children to disobey. As far as possible, however, we should remove from their way occasions for making mistakes.

In every situation of life a child is striving in his own distinct and individual way, to overcome difficulty. If the difficulty springs from the mistaken attitude of the child's parents or the other children in the family, the child will always show, in actions how the child tries to overcome difficulty. The degree of social interest that the child has acquired in family life will also be apparent.

The child's actions will reveal how the child feels toward other family members. Whatever we find to blame in problem children comes from their lack of interest in the life of the family. They do not feel themselves an equal part of the family. They cannot cooperate. Such a child, therefore, always presents the picture of egotism.

There can be no doubt of this when we find a child who acts the part of a tyrant, who is arrogant or destructive, or who lies, steals, or plays truant. It is quite clear that this is a fighting child. The child is fighting for his or her own interests and against the family and all others. The child is not a part of the whole. This child feels that he or she must play a lone hand against the environment. It may be more difficult to see this when the child's behavior is more passive

If a child is lazy, timid, bashful, reserved or untidy, we do not see the child's goal of egotism on the surface. Nevertheless, all these characteristics reveal that the child does not feel equal to others, and is not interested in contributing to the common welfare of the family or the school. Even obedience may be a sign of egotism. It may be used when parents are severe or as a means of avoiding trouble and difficulties. Some pampered children exaggerate obedience as a means of winning their parents' appreciation and reward.

The best development for a child comes when the child can feel that he or she is a part of the family life and is able to consider the other members. If the child is interested in others, the child's striving for superiority will be united with social feeling. The child will act courageously and optimistically on the useful side of life.

Commentary:
Behavior is governed by reason or by mistakes in reason. The mistakes of childhood are those which direct behavior in useless directions. Gentle reasoning is more useful than admonitions. Child rearing requires us to guide children toward cooperative endeavors. Cooperation is not to be confused with compliance. Compliance infers obedience. Cooperation asks for joint effort and agreement. Wise parents model cooperation and show children how to meet life's challenges.

10

School Problems

This lecture was given at the Institute for Advanced Education in New York City, on 24 October 1933. Dr. Adler reiterates the importance of teaching children courage and cooperation.

When a child enters school for the first time, the child is faced with a wholly new experience. Like many new situations, this activity is an exam, it will show us how the child faces new challenges. There are many differences in the way that children approach school. Some are well-prepared. Others are not prepared at all. If we could record the child's approach to school, we would gain an understanding of the child's ability to meet new situations.

Later in life, many people hesitate or stop when they are faced with new situations. It would be very illuminating to know how these individuals prepared for nursery school, elementary school, etc. School is a task requiring cooperation with teachers and peers. If a child is interested in anything, it should be explored. When a child indicates that he or she is not interested in anything, this tells us that the child is not rightly prepared for new situations. The child's attendance, attitude, posture, willingness to listen and sit still are indicative of the child's degree of interest. Pampered children express no interest.

When teachers encourage pampered children to participate, the children become very good pupils. They excel when they have an advantage. However, we cannot always guarantee this advantage. If the child changes schools, the child may stop because the child is accustomed to having everything easy. The child is not prepared to face new situations and difficulties.

Report cards carry much weight. Too much emphasis is given to subjects. I do not undervalue subjects, but I encourage teachers to teach subjects in coherence so that children see the purpose and practical value of the subject. This is a great problem. Do we teach the child to learn subjects, or do we educate the child? In some schools, teachers combine subjects in a way that fosters the children's interest. It is a very worthwhile presupposition that a teacher is interested in the children.

In regard to the education of children, it should be acknowledged that children are in personal competition. Some children are pushed ahead and others are not. This creates great rivalry in the classroom. Ambitious children do not like others to get ahead. They are not well-prepared for cooperation. We must teach children cooperation not competition. The classroom is a unit. Each child should feel like a part of the whole.

Children know who is best at spelling, arithmetic, drawing, athletics, etc. They classify each other. They may not be just, but they know it and esteem it. It is a mistaken view. They limit themselves believing 'I can never catch up.' When a child fixes an opinion, the opinion transfers to adult life. The individual will stop rather than develop potentialities. A great majority of children go through school expressing the same level of interest. Their interest is always in the average range. This is not due to intelligence, but due to limits the child has created. This can be changed. Children must be encouraged to face new challenges with courage.

It is important to find out where the child's interests lie. If the teacher finds out which subjects interest a child, the teacher can guide the child to success. With success the child will be encouraged to try new things. If the child feels appreciated, it will be easier to stimulate the child's interest in new areas. It is useful to find out which sense organ the child prefers. Some children are trained in looking, others in listening and others in moving. If you find a child who prefers visual stimulation, you will see that this child excels in geography and so on. This child will not do as well listening to the teacher.

We should rid ourselves of the superstition that intelligence is the result of heredity. Some parents and teachers say that a child's poor academic performance is due to heredity. This releases the adults and the children from any responsibility. It would be wrong to say that heredity does not play a part in academic performance. We would be wise to gain an understanding of the way that deficiencies in heredity affect the mind. Individual Psychology insists that the mind experiences the degree of each organ's ability to perform. Heredity is only an expression of the ability of the brain. The brain can be trained and it will compensate.

If a child has bad report cards and is not beloved by the teacher, the child suffers. School is a burden for this child. Very often, when this child is at home, the child is criticized, reproached, scolded and spanked. The parents do not treat the child nicely. This is too much. Before the report cards are given, teachers must consider what will happen to the child at home. Will the child be treated cruelly at home? If so, the child may not go home after receiving a bad report card. Sometimes under these conditions, children commit suicide. When this happens, teachers should not be blamed. These children were poorly prepared for school. If the teacher had looked into the child's family life and the teacher had been benevolent, the child may have been encouraged to perform well in school.

Children who always go home with bad report cards may believe that they are the worst pupils in school. If I were in their shoes, and always had bad report cards, I would not like school. I would try to escape. We should not be upset when these children prefer to skip school. When adolescents skip school there is cause for concern. Adolescents are clever. They hide on streets where they cannot be seen and they meet other children. They may become gang members. It is wrong to believe that a child is hopeless. Following the lessons of Individual Psychology, adults can find methods to help discouraged children. Discouraged children can improve, even in the worst circumstances.

If you observe the way that a child enters school, you will see the child's style of life. When you understand children, you can successfully educate them. Overcrowded classrooms must be avoided. It is important for the teacher to know all of the pupils. It is also a benefit to the child, if the child has the same teacher from year to year.

Some people say that we should promote outstanding and prominent children. I do not agree with this. Prominent children might help slower children. It seems like there are two classes of children in school. There are prominent children who have been well-prepared for school and there are slower children who tend to be from poor families. It tells me that among poor families the parents are confronted with too many concerns and they are not able to devote their time to preparing the children for school. I do not believe that prominent children and children of the poor should be in separate classes. I believe that they can learn from one another and that all children can be encouraged to excel academically.

Sex education in the schools is a complicated problem. School is not the right place for sex education. It is better to speak with each child individually. If the teacher speaks to the whole class, the teacher will not know if the children understand. It is different if the children want to know and ask privately. We should not make a bagatelle out of sex.

I want to remind you about the unity of the individual. Here we see the greatest common denominator. If a child is lying, the child has lost courage. The child is making a detour. If a child disrupts the classroom, we see a child who likes to take the lead role, but does not lead in a useful way. If we see a child experiencing problems in school, we know that the child was not properly prepared for school. When this happens, we must teach the child cooperation and help the child meet new situations with courage.

Commentary:

A child's approach to school reflects the child's approach to life. School is "the life of the child." Some children arrive at school prepared to learn because they feel like they can handle new situations. Other children arrive at school less prepared. They have not been encouraged to face new situations with courage. They are likely to experience difficulty in school. These children need understanding and assistance. Patient reasoning is a recommended approach. With encouragement, all students can learn to meet new situations with courage and reach their potential.

11

Stuttering

This lecture was presented to the Long Island College of Medicine on 30 November 1932. Dr. Adler explains the importance of cooperation in communication.

As we consider stuttering, we must look at cooperation and resistance to cooperation. Language is a connection between two or more persons requiring cooperation. Stuttering is a retreat from cooperation because the individual who stutters does not cooperate in speaking. We cannot assume that stuttering is based on an organic deficiency.

Song birds of a certain kind sing differently if they are raised by another species of birds. Like song birds, we find that the expression of voice, tone and language is the creation of the individual. It is not a gift of nature. The way in which the child creates these expressions is important. The riddle is why some persons do not develop speech in the right way.

Perhaps we solve this riddle by finding out what is gained. Naturally, this individual gives a certain task to others. Maybe this individual wants attention. Maybe this individual wants to be supported by others. Such individuals are pampered or they wish to be. Generally, stutterers are pampered children. When you are convinced of this, our inquiries are simplified.

Although there are always varieties and nuances among stutterers, you will always find that the basic mistake is that the stutterer wants to be supported by others. When children are learning to speak, at least 40 percent show signs of stuttering. This occurs because the child has not yet fully developed all of the nerve fibers needed for speech. Children have some defects and they are sensitive to the way in which others listen to them speak. As they grow, most children stop stuttering. However, some children continue to stutter. When you see this, you will understand that the child found a way to gain attention. The child continues this way because it seems to be the best way to gain superiority. They are always backed by others and they always have extenuating circumstances. Stuttering gives the family a new task.

If the pampered child were rid of this problem, the child would make trouble in other ways. Telling the child about the purpose of the symptom will not diminish the problem. The child will not understand. The child has built up a life style during a time when the child did not connect a truth with words and did not have the words to verbalize it.

We must remember that speaking does not indicate thinking first. It is a very funny expression that people tell stutterers to think first and then speak. I do not believe that anyone does this. Speaking is an expression of the whole. The tongue is a very intelligent tool in many ways. It is admirable that in chewing we do not bite the tongue and that the tongue always makes the right movements in chewing and speaking. This is the result of evolution. We must trust that our speech organs contain a certain intelligence, that they express what we want to and that they are able to arrive at a goal which is leading our movements.

Stutterers always try to think before they speak. They are misled. They look at speech as if it were the most important part of living. If we focus on one part of life too much, the harmony of our life is destroyed. Life is harmony. As the body strives for equilibrium, each function is necessary. All of the body's organs work together in such a complicated way that we never know where the beginning was. When there is illness, we hardly know where to start. It is the same in the mind. If a person has artificially led our attention to a certain point of focus, this harmony is destroyed. In the mind, harmony and striving for equilibrium are also destroyed. One part of the mind which can never be exaggerated or over emphasized is social interest.

I would like to draw attention to the idea that stuttering is associated with feeblemindedness. This is a mistake. To create symptoms of stuttering is an art. Stuttering is a symptom that is in harmony with the individual's whole style of life. It is a creation of the individual. Feebleminded individuals cannot create. Therefore, it is useless to test for feeblemindedness. The stutterer may have a low IQ, but the stutterer is not feebleminded. Stutterers cannot answer rightly. They are on retreat. People who retreat from others, do not answer rightly.

Stutterers like talking. Talking becomes a prominent task. Sometimes you will find a stutterer who was a great orator as in the case of Demosthenes. Each case must be considered unique and specific to the individual. You must investigate how the individual utilizes the symptom. Many people who would never stutter do so when they are alarmed. Certain personalities are more inclined to stuttering than others. In all cases, the individual has some backing which encourages the stuttering to continue. The stutterer must be backed, supported, encouraged, favored and appreciated. This what the stutterer wants.

If the stutterer cooperates in language, this individual would connect with others. Emotions hold the stutterer back. Stutterers fear they will not be appreciated or valued by others. This perspective toward life is different from what we would normally expect. Stuttering is a symptom of the individual's feelings. It is better to speak about neurotic symptoms than to classify. Some experts classify stuttering as an anxiety neurosis. Others classify stuttering as a compulsion neurosis. You will see how they explain it. Stuttering differs from both in appearance and structure.

We do not have one rule, one short sentence to characterize the structure of stuttering. You will find special symptoms that do not fit every case of stuttering. To classify stuttering as we classify other neuroses, would be difficult. In the basis of this structure we always find anxiety, but this anxiety is not expressed. You will find this anxiety or feeling of inferiority in all neurotic cases.

You may find a certain amount of resistance. If things do not go the way that the client wishes, the client may be lost and feel like an inferior being. When the client stutters, others assist. In this way the client is the center of attention. The only way to help this client is to encourage the client to express social interest.

If the client resists the therapist's explanation, the client is in a trap. The client must prove that the therapist is wrong. The client has to prove that the therapist is not right, otherwise, the client has to change. This is a very important dynamic. The client has to prove that he or she is not leaning on anyone, even though the therapist sees it. The client has to prove that he or she is not utilizing stuttering as an extenuating circumstance. If the stuttering client does not resist, or the resistance is not great, then the therapist can convince the client. In this way the therapist has an advantage on two sides.

To be successful with this patient, the therapist must favor and appreciate the client. Otherwise, the patient will not connect with the therapist. You see, this little part of social interest, interest in the other person must be utilized. The therapist has to explain everything in a patient and friendly manner so that the client understands. Go slowly, do not hurry. If the client resists, do not express anger. If the client starts to speak rightly, the client will lose equilibrium in the rear. The client must always be encouraged, never scolded. The best way to assist the client is to avoid addressing the client's stuttering. It is better to explain the mistaken style of life regarding all the events of the past and of the present using the client's earliest recollections.

Commentary:
Stuttering is a complex phenomenon. There are many theories for its origins and its treatment. Adler ascribes some of its manifestation to pampering whereby the child has learned to perpetuate the phenomenon as a means of gaining attention. This behavior is in harmony with the individual's life style.

Communication is a form of cooperation. If we look at stuttering in relation to the individual's life style, it is likely that the individual has not been adequately trained to cooperate with others. Adler argues that understanding the goals of the behavior, in this case stuttering, will better prepares us for dealing honestly with the condition. As with other conditions, we must ask, "what is the purpose of the behavior?"

12

Adolescence

This lecture was given on 9 December 1929 at Community Church in New York City and transcribed by Alan Porter. Dr. Adler discusses the challenges of adolescence and emphasizes the importance of courage and cooperation.

In our society, children are taken care of and protected by their parents. In adolescence, children are beginning to face the time when they must take care of themselves. This is the reason why adolescence can be difficult. If it is difficult, faulty development is revealed.

If a child has not been properly trained and prepared for independence, the child will shrink from the task of adult life. The child continues to ask for pampering and support. In adolescence, some children feel that they are nearing the battle front of life and they fall into a panic. For these children, to be responsible for themselves, to be helpful and supportive of others seems to be a harsh and impossible demand.

There are many ways of expressing such a panic. Some discouraged children will hit everyone around them. They will quarrel with parents and adults. They will generally make a nuisance of themselves. Other children will sulk, stop all activities, and act as if there were a magic circle holding them back. Both types are responding in their own characteristic manner to a situation which they feel is dangerous.

Many people are frightened of adolescence. They regard it as a special and peculiar crisis. Hundreds of books have been written on the awful perils lying in wait for the adolescent, but, adolescence is not a crisis. It is a phase of development, like any other phase. It never produces a change of character, though it often brings to the surface mistakes that had previously passed without notice.

During adolescence there are new situations to meet and every new situations call for new efforts of adaptation. For almost every youth, adolescence means one thing above all others. The child must prove that he or she is no longer a child.

Naturally, if the child feels that proof is needed, the child will exaggerate the point. If the child took for granted the fact that he or she was no longer a child, the child would not draw attention to the matter. If the child is not quite sure, the child will fight for the right to be considered grown up.

If the child feels that being grown up means being free from control, the child will fight against restrictions. During adolescence, many children begin to smoke, drink, swear and stay out all night. In such conduct they are imitating what they feel are the privileges of adulthood. Generally, children are given more freedom during adolescence. Parents no longer feel that they need to watch over them and guard them all the time. If, however, parents try to continue their supervision, the child will make stronger efforts to assert independence. It is in these cases that we get the picture of 'adolescent negativism', where every suggestion is resented and every cooperation refused.

During adolescence the organs of the body are developing and sometimes coordination of the functions is not easily accomplished. Children grow taller. Their hands and feet grow larger. The process is not always harmonious. Perhaps they are less active and skillful. If the adolescent is laughed at for their temporary clumsiness, they may come to believe that they can never be anything but clumsy.

At this time, we sometimes see apparent reversals of progress. Children who were brilliant pupils in school begin to seem slow and stupid. They do not fulfill their early promise. Other children who seemed less talented begin to overtake them. This is not really in contradiction to the previous history. The brilliant children who now fall behind were spoilt children. They could only make such a fine showing when they were helped and appreciated. As time comes for these children to make independent efforts, their courage fails. They feel that they can never realize their ambitions.

We also find that some adolescents are stimulated by their new freedom. The road to the fulfillment of their hopes is clearly before them. New ideas and new projects fill their minds. Their interest in all parts of human culture broadens and increases. New abilities are discovered. Their creative desires find new opportunities for exercise. For these children, no period of life can be more interesting and lovely. They seem to be living in the springtime of life. They are courageous children, who are interested, not in themselves, but in others. In their earliest years they were prepared to meet new situations with confidence and independence. They do not look on adult life as offering hardships and dangers, but as giving fresh opportunities for work and contribution.

Commentary:

The transition from childhood to adulthood continues the process of individual responsibility. Children who have been raised to progressively assume responsibility and personal independence make the transition with relative ease. Children who have not achieved sufficient independence and responsibility on their own, must either wrest it from controlling parents or quake from its sudden arrival. In the latter case, adolescents may find the transition filled with great difficulty. They may become discouraged if their feelings of self confidence and acceptance wane. Peer pressure may add to feelings of inferiority and insecurity. Re-education can introduce new ways of coping with life's challenges and help adolescents correct their misperceptions.

13

The Approach to Womanhood

This lecture was transcribed by Alan Porter. The date and occasion are unknown. Dr. Adler talks about feminine roles. He addresses culturally imposed inequality between the sexes and encourages democracy.

Women have the same problems as men. Both men and women must train themselves to be cooperative members of society; then they will find a successful way through life. They must engage in work which contributes to the welfare of others. They must be good friends to other human beings. They must be true and equal partners in love. Anyone who fulfills these three tasks will never be faced with overwhelming difficulties.

The solution of the three tasks of life has been very much complicated by the superstition that women are somehow inferior to men. Even today women's work and women's worth are almost always under-rated. On the whole, only the tasks which have fallen to men are given serious attention.

There could be no higher task, for example than the task of motherhood. There is no greater art. Nothing demands more interest, more skill or intelligence. Yet, today, motherhood is still insufficiently valued. Many people are found who idealize motherhood, but few afford it equal recognition to 'masculine' pursuits. Perhaps we see evidence for this view of motherhood in the fact that our society does not recognize motherhood as a profession deserving economic return.

If men are ranked higher than women and boys are preferred over girls, it need not surprise us that many girls feel discontent with their role. They do not look forward to being women. They feel that they have been given a bad deal. As they approach womanhood, their dislike for their feminine role becomes more obvious. They have a pessimistic view of the opportunities that the feminine role offers.

Among girls who exaggerate the importance of being a man, we see many varieties of behavior. Sometimes we see only a dislike of the other sex. Other times we see girls who like boys well enough, but feel embarrassed when they are with boys. These girls do not enjoy speaking with boys. They feel ill at ease with sexuality. Often they insist that they wish to marry when they are older, but they do not approach boys and form no friendships with boys.

Some adolescent girls actively express their discouragement and dislike of the feminine role. They behave more boyishly than before. They attempt to imitate boys and they are drawn to male vices: smoking, drinking, swearing, joining gangs, or displaying sexual freedom.

Girls will compensate for the greater degree of seriousness with which boys are treated. This compensation is seen in a very unfortunate way. In some families, girls are petted and pampered more often than boys. Pampering anyone is a means of treating the individual as if he or she were inferior and incapable of looking out for himself or herself. If a girl is brought up in a family of boys, it almost invariably happens that she is both petted and teased. She may conclude that no one will ever take her seriously.

Some girls who have been pampered, are hypnotized by their craving for appreciation. It is dangerous for girls, as well as, boys to look only for praise. If girls have low self confidence, they may seek the approval of others as a means of proving their worth. Such girls easily fall prey to those who understand how to flatter them. I have known girls who felt unappreciated by their parents and siblings. As these girls became women, they started to have love affairs as means of achieving a position where they could be the centers of attention. These women under-rate their feminine role.

We find that dissatisfaction with the feminine role is not a new development in adolescence. The child's discomfort was seen in early childhood. In these early years the child indicated dissatisfaction with the position of girls and thought it more enviable to be a boy. Some girls wear boys' clothes or play boys' games. It is comparatively rare that we see a boy who acts as if he were a girl. From this, we may guess how frequently it is supposed that the male role in life is better than the female role in life. As girls approach womanhood, they may rebel openly to inequality. If men and women are comrades and not enemies, their equality must be unconditionally recognized. Girls should never have cause to regret that they are girls and boys should not be granted superior privileges.

Commentary:
Adler addresses challenges women face relative to gender stereotypes. Among those challenges is the age old belief that men are accorded rights and privileges that are not

accorded to women. As women become aware of cultural inequalities, they may become discouraged about their role in society. Adler acknowledges these inequalities. He promotes appreciation for the role of motherhood and encourages cooperation between the sexes.

14

The Approach to Manhood

This lecture was transcribed by Alan Porter. The date and occasion are unknown. Dr. Adler talks about male roles. He addresses the importance of equality between the sexes and encourages cooperation.

Boys, as well as, girls overate the importance of 'being a man' and then suffer the consequence. Our whole civilization gives first place to men. This situation can be difficult for boys. If they are not quite sure of themselves, they will see masculinity as an ideal which they are not strong enough to achieve.

There are different ways of showing their fear of the role. Some boys will be under tension all the time to prove that they are masculine. Others will try to avoid any test of their masculinity because they fear they will be proved wanting.

The caveman of popular fiction is really a man who thinks that he is not manly enough. If he isn't asserting his strength all the time, he will feel weak and inferior. However, the very writers who romanticize this type are the ones who show insight into the cowardice that lies beneath. The caveman is afraid that if his masculinity were put to the test, he would prove inadequate.

Therefore, some boys who want to be manly struggle vigorously to convince themselves that they are men. These boys are compelled to caricature the qualities of masculinity. They think that to be a man means to be "hard-boiled." They never give way. They always keep the upper hand. They even see love as a conquest, not as an equal partnership and a common task.

If an individual's goal is to dominate and rule over others, the individual will not have an easy time adjusting to society. Society's first demand is cooperation. It has no room for people who are mainly interested in proving their personal superiority.

Often a boy who has a delicate or 'feminine' appearance has an especially difficult time. When he is a child, strangers may ask him, 'Are you a boy or girl?' Even friends of the family may say, 'You really should have been a girl.' The child's classmates may make fun of him or bully him. Such a child is very apt in later life to take his appearance as a sign of insufficiency. He may regard solving the problems of love and marriage as too hard.

Often boys who are not sure that they can acquit themselves well as men, tend to imitate girls during their adolescence. They become effeminate and act like girls who have been pampered. They act coquettish, posing and cultivating a temperament. They feel that too much is demanded of their sex. They want to take refuge.

It is always more difficult for a boy who experiences a domineering mother. He will grow up expecting women to try to dominate him. He will always be on the lookout for such attempts. He will think that holding his own with women calls for an extraordinary degree of effort. Such circumstances are not at all favorable for inducing a feeling of ease and comradeship with the other sex.

The case is made worse for a child who is the only boy in a family of girls. Often the girls will unite to criticize him and to prevent him from taking advantage of the fact that he is a boy. He grows-up in a feminine atmosphere. The whole home is probably tidier and less noisy than if there were other boys about. Therefore, this young man may seem to have more 'feminine' traits and interests than other boys. He may strongly resent the attempt of any woman to influence him. Nietzsche was in this situation. All his life he exaggerated the power of women and the necessity to avoid being influenced by them.

Children should never be left in doubt of their sex. By the time they are two years old they should know quite definitely whether or not they are boys or girls. Otherwise, they may carry with them through life some doubt of what is expected of them. Children should also be trained to accept the advantages and disadvantages of their role as part of our present culture. They should not regard their role as a sign of personal merit or personal inferiority.

Above all, boys and girls should learn from their earliest childhood to cooperate together in friendship and equality. The more they are in friendly contact with each other in early life, the easier they will find it to respect one another and get along when they are grown up. Successful marriages are only possible for those who have learned to cooperate. In reality, true manhood and true womanhood call for the same qualities. They require courage to face the problems of life, social feeling, independent and optimistic effort, the ability to be interested others, to give rather than receive and to ask for no special privileges or special consideration.

Commentary:
Having addressed gender related stereotypes and female roles, Adler now considers male roles. Some males may perceive their role in society as if they are superior to women. They believe that they will be accorded rights and privileges that are not accorded to women. These men may act out these misperceptions by overplaying their "manly" role. The result produces conflicts and not cooperation. It creates the perception of superior and inferior status. Such misperceptions complicate gender relationships and perpetuate gender related myths. Boys and girls must learn to cooperate in order to grow into responsible adult roles. Children who fail to learn cooperation, have difficulty as adults.

15

Future of Love

The date and occasion and transcription of this lecture are unknown. Dr. Adler addresses fortune telling and the notion of a perfect love. He emphasizes love as a task for two.

There are only two ways to predict. One way is to see what a person or nation possesses, and then apply what has been discovered in the past, vaguely or distinctly, to the problem as it appears today. Many persons dwell on these purposes and enterprises. They look for the future in superficial comparisons, in questioning cards, in palmistry, in horoscopes and in other kinds of fortune telling. Often persons engaged in these enterprises acquire a profound experience in regard to people who consult them and are able, being guided by slight impressions, gestures, play of features and expressions to guess what others who are not so trained could not guess so well. The predictions given to their customers are not merely empty words; they arouse emotions and tendencies to bring about what has been predicted.

Of greater value we find some of the predictions of graphologists, physiognomists [sic] and experimental psychologists. We are justified in doubting in these cases how much their judgment influences the person in question, sometimes giving strong limits, sometimes enhancing efforts that have been made before. All predictions of this kind (fall in a stream of consciousness) act as a stimulating contribution, a way of striving to conquer problems. Much more modest, but more effective, are the predictions combined with an 'if.' Considering the development of the human race, historians, economists, politicians, and parents, teachers, and psychologists—should always regard this 'if.' They should not expect anything to happen or disappear without distinct effort, but should show the goal which could be reached 'if' we could use our human power in the best way.

The greatest part of human progress has been brought about because of intolerable need. As this need could not be avoided, the human race swung from one extreme to the other, seeking equilibrium, a compromise between two mistakes, both of which contained some advantages. There is no question that this is the usual course of uncontrolled development. This oscillation back and forth could be partly lessened 'if' our understanding of human life and its meaning could be increased. The equilibrium between humans and their environment can never be entirely obtained. Nevertheless, our striving for the right answer is an eternal one. We seek only a better understanding of our goal and how to accomplish happiness in our social life.

It is more or less understood that everyone's success in life is dependent upon the growing welfare of the human race. To arrive at a higher level, all our personal problems have to be looked upon as problems of the human race. The problem of love, the basic problem of propagating and educating of children to be fellow beings, presents the question like a mathematical task. We have to answer it the best way, stimulated and led by sexuality and social interest, attracted bodily and mentally by persons of the other sex. We can say the fate of the human race is in the hands of each man and each woman. Therefore, love is not only a happy personal situation and feeling, but also a task calling for an improvement of life and a task not for one, but for two persons to accomplish together.

The task for these two persons is a unifying process which can only be accomplished with a strict agreement. From the beginning, this agreement must exclude any doubt of each other, any protest against each other, any protest against love and its implications. The main tasks which must be carried out, must be mutual devotion, mutual trust, mutual interest. These qualities can be obtained and sustained only by complete agreement and a final decision. Each individual must feel a part of this joint undertaking and must help.

We cannot count on an idea of perfection to eliminate counteracting tendencies on both sides. The numerous unhappy love affairs and broken marriages always show that it has not been understood that marriage is a task for two persons in a decision of finality. We must learn this lesson for the sake of the future. Of course it is much easier for persons trained from the beginning of life in cooperation to solve the problem of love. The right attitude in regard to love can be seen in an ability to make friends and to keep friendship, to stick to one's job, which means cooperation, and to be persistent in it and to be more interested in the welfare of one's love-partner than one's self.

Poets, more so than the average person, are moved by the distress of love. Unhappy love relationships are the usual problems of their writings. Artists have always been the inspiring leaders of the human race. They have felt the vibrations of our social life. There is no doubt that in agreement with the poets sentiments, love in our time is going to be a more complicated problem confronting us with higher demands. This is because we put it on a higher level and endow it with higher feelings than before. In our current time, love is a task which needs better preparation than the old traditional one. Perhaps one of the reasons may be that procreation is no more such an inciting motive, and housekeeping no longer the unavoidable occupation for women.

The central point of love rises higher in the sphere of feelings and emotions in the unity of men and women and finds a generation not rightly prepared for the task that requires cooperation by two persons. The average man expects an easy superiority in a traditional way. Women of today are educated. Women are striving for equality, which is more or less already in the conscious mind of the people. Progress offers women freedom from housework and a different place in the unit of love. The question now becomes, in a more or less strict sense, is love to be luxury or comradeship? After many mistakes have been made in love relations, the desire for more subtle feelings is enforced by expiring old traditions. The answer is comradeship in just equality.

The question of beauty will also be answered more fittingly. Now, more than before, health and natural selection follow the way of hygiene. This course seems inevitable. The increase of knowledge, understanding and social responsibility is slowly being extorted by a growing need, and the importance of these matters will be taught from childhood.

Those who lower the level of love, and those who experiment with it and make a trifle of it, are doomed. Their actions are recognized as expressions of an inferiority complex. The future of love will be based upon social responsibility, equality, mutual devotion and a final decision. Those who express a stronger accord with human welfare and a better understanding of human nature will be able to distinguish between an inevitable dissolution of love and curable obstacles. They will also be able to place more social responsibility in the start of the union.

Commentary:
The welfare of society is dependent upon the future of love. Adler speaks of the deepest love where individuals allow themselves the risk of feeling truly vulnerable. Those who express the courage to love promote the future of cooperative society. Adler's conception of love is that of the Greek ἀγάπη *(agape) which expresses a feeling of one-*

ness with others. This expression of love is in keeping with Adler's attention to a spirit of cooperation that must abound if society is to grow.

16

The Family Life

This speech was given on 25 November 1929 at Community Church in New York City. This is one in a series of free public lectures given at the Church by Alfred Adler. Dr. Adler talks about the importance of family in preparing children for life.

The main view of Individual psychology is the importance of the whole coherence of our social life. Social life demands and forces an organization in which children are raised and prepared for later life. All other organizations (orphanages, boarding houses, institutions) are only substitutes for family. They replace the influence of the mother and the father. Therefore, the best way to raise children is to provide good family life. It is important for the future of the human race.

The best family life is one that is not shaken by anything. The parents are adjusted to marriage and family. They are united. The children will not find dissension between the parents. The parents must educate the children toward social life so that the children grow up to be independent and cooperative. We look for cooperation between the parents. The parents must look for their marriage and family life as eternity. Monogamy is the right evolution in marriage. Great difficulties in marriage arise when individuals are not rightly trained in cooperation. If the parents are of this type, they are always looking for an escape. This will influence the children. Children are always for monogamy.

Cooperation between the parents creates equality. This is important in educating the children. Each member of the family should feel they are an equal part. The parents must be involved in this striving for equality. One partner must not play a lesser role. The wife must not give in to the husband. The husband is mistaken to believe that his wife is a servant. The husband must try to live with her in an equal manner. He must acquaint her with his ideas and goals. He must give her a place for her own development. Then there will be satisfaction in the family and they can truly cooperate. Cooperation is not possible if one partner feels inferior.

Children must feel that they are a part of the whole. When parents are truly cooperative and socially adjusted, they do not suppress others. From the beginning, parents role model social behavior. Then there are no difficulties unless there are great mistakes. Little mistakes can always be corrected. If there are great mistakes they appear when children act peevish and lazy and when children do not join others or help others. If children feel that they are apart of the whole they will realize their own responsibility. They like it and enjoy working together. When this happens, we do not see a children striving for superiority by trying to rule and boss the others. In a family where the ideal of equality prevails, children do not learn to fight or suppress others and the great rivalry among children disappears.

Another mistake in family life occurs when one member behaves as a prominent person and uses authority. This will always create feelings of inferiority for others. If individuals are always looking up, they will always feel belittled. It is a mistake for one individual to show superiority by acting as a ruling authority. We cannot avoid it. One member of the family will be prominent, but this prominence must not suppress others. The family must get rid of superiority where it is treated as if it were inherited, blessed or a special talent. If there is this type of superiority in the family others will revolt. If the parents use authority to suppress their children, the children will feel insecure and in some cases they may rebel. No one wants to be subjugated. It hinders social life.

Difficulty in married life appears when one partner is the conqueror. This is not permitted and the fighting begins. The last result is divorce. In every disturbed marriage we see mistakes that can be corrected. Many marriages start in a mistaken way. Divorce results as a consequence of mistakes made in the very beginning of the marriage. Marriage is a task for two persons. It can only be accomplished when there is comradeship.

Family life is like trees growing together. Some grow more quickly and overshadow the others. While one grows quickly, the others are stopped. Parents should not promote one child. No child should be the favorite. Children always find out who is preferred and they resist it. The overshadowed children develop egocentric attitudes and are more interested in their own person than in others. It is very obvious. It is human nature. Everyone who feels deprived or belittled wants more. They may find relief in a useless way such as fighting or they may become hopeless, discouraged or delinquent. When these children face life's challenges, they seek relief. They are pessimistic. These children do not expect to be equal or prominent because they have discovered that others are more favored. It is difficult for parents not to favor a bright child. They must encourage the child to participate cooperatively with others.

There are other mistakes in family life that must be considered. One of the greatest mistakes is that when a child becomes sick, a parent expresses fear. Parents should not show children that they are worried. Children find an easy way to impress the parents. Children may not look well, they may feel sick, they may not eat rightly and they may complain in all their functions. In this way, children find themselves in the center of attention. Parents must not over stress a certain special interest. If a child wants to be the center of attention, as a great majority of children do, you will see that children use the parent's special interest to control the parents.

In some families, cleanliness is over stressed. If a child in this family wants to worry the parents and fight against them, the child will find being dirty the greatest pleasure in life. This is especially true in families where the child is carried a great deal. This creates a pampered child and conditions the whole adult life of the individual. The individual expects to be the center of attention. This child is not trained for working alone. The child may hesitate or stop when faced with certain problems. This behavior is seen when the child attends school. Parents should not over stress the importance of school. If children find school to be a natural development and not a nuisance or a difficulty, they will not attempt to be the centers of attention in school. They will not corrupt the class.

I am often asked how to raise children so that they express cooperation. I will give you some practical hints that should be used in the beginning of the child's life. The whole family should be together at meal time, especially at breakfast. In our society where activities begin at eight or nine, the family should sit down for breakfast at seven. Everyone should be completely dressed. The children will become accustomed to getting up early and sharing with others. Meals should be harmonious times, with no one reading the paper. Everyone should contribute to the congenial atmosphere. If children lay around in bed until 11:00 a.m. or Noon when they are not even sleepy, they will be inclined to stay out all night can come home late when they are teenagers. Therefore, family breakfast is very important.

The differences between children within the family do not spring from inheritances, but the way in which children understand their individual positions within the family. Whether the child is the oldest, the second, or the youngest, each child grows-up in a unique position within the family. Each child has a different place in the family. This creates tension between them.

The oldest child can be alone and very pampered. The oldest child tends to be the center of attention until the birth of a sibling, then the oldest child is dethroned and has lost a favored position. It may be hard to convince the child to cooperate. If the child is one or two years old, the parents cannot argue with the child because the child will experience this as a great burden. The child may feel deprived and experience the birth of the sibling as an unjust tragedy.

The oldest child may develop jealousy and look at the newborn as an enemy. After awhile, the oldest child may begin fighting. The birth of the sibling brings feelings of humiliation. The child may pull the mother to his/her side attempting to gain the mother's attention. When the oldest acts on good behavior, the mother will be pleased and will hardly notice the child's effort. However, problem behavior that disrupts the household will get the mother's attention. She will be kept busy with the child's misbehavior. In this way, the oldest child may regain a sense of power and continue as the center of attention. As this individual goes through life, the individual will be suspicious if others do not dethrone him/her. In this way, the oldest child is always posed to fight.

The second child is always a pacemaker and is irritated by the older child. The second child must wear the clothing of the oldest child and the second child resists. The second child is always striving to catch up with the first. This striving forms the second child's whole style of life. The second child is always in a race, as if someone should be counting for them. This can be exaggerated and used for bad purposes. It is very hard to make these two children cooperate. This is a task and an art. I very much doubt that most parents do it rightly.

In the situation of the youngest child, you see a great difference. The youngest child is never alone like the oldest. The youngest has no follower like the oldest or the second child. Youngest children are more pampered than all the others, because there is always a pacemaker ahead of the youngest child, you will see that the youngest is like the second born in some ways. The youngest is in a better situation than the second, but is trying to run over all the others. You often find that the youngest child takes the cake. This is true in all ages. You see it in the Bible and in fairy tales. The youngest child tries to catch up and meets someone who cannot be conquered. What will the child do with an exaggerated striving to be on top? The child turns to the useless side and is in danger of becoming a problem child. The child loses hope.

The greatest difficulty in life of an oldest boy is to be followed by a younger sister. If the number of years between them is not very great, then the boy may become weak. The tension between these two is the same as the tension between any two children, but the girl is highly motivated to prove that she is equal.

Nature favors girls during the first 16 years of life. Girls mature intellectually and physically sooner than boys. The oldest boy may feel defeated.

Courage is important. It means to be cooperative. In cooperation you will always feel as if you are a part of the whole. You will feel like you are at home on the planet earth. You will have courage and will not look only for advantages in life, but you will find pleasure in solving life's difficulties. We must look to the future of the human race. We must train our children to take up their burdens with courage. They must not be discouraged. They must compete and work in a cooperative manner.

I am always asked how many children there should be in a family. As I shall probably receive this question, I will answer it now. And I shall discuss the only child. An only child is trained to be the center of attention. Later, social life is very difficult for this child. Social life will seem an enmity. It is like going out to the glass house for a plant and you face the rough, cold air. The only child will always be surprised and disappointed. The only child will need courage to overcome this difficulty. Many children overcome it, but we should not be surprised to see discouraged only children.

In regard to the number of children there should be in a family, I would advise as is convenient. No matter the number of children, whether there are many or only one, there will be certain problems that arise. In our culture and our social life, a family should have 3–5 children with three years between children. This gives the best situation. At three years of age, parents can explain and lead the child. If a child comes after one year, the older child will feel dethroned. You cannot explain to the child or convince the child to cooperate, feelings of inferiority consume the child. If the distance between children is greater than five years, you have two only children. The first child is an only for five years and then another child arrives.

I doubt that we can train, educate and teach all parents that they should look for their problems in marriage and in the family and that these problems can be solved. I believe that there should be an institution of selected experts who can truly answer parents' questions about marriage, family education, etc.

The education of children is important. It is not enough to learn history but it is more important to learn how to look for history. It is not enough to learn mathematics, but these tasks should be applied to our social life. The schools need to teach this. School is really a prolonged hand of the family. It increases the social life. If families were able to raise children to social life, school would be superficial. Family life prepares children for school life. School life educates the children for social life. Everyone should know what to do. I want to stress the importance of school in correcting the mistakes made in family life.

Teachers have to be elevated and should be of greater importance and play a higher role than they do now. It is the work of the teachers to find the right way to correct the mistakes made in the family before the child enters the social life of school. Many problems could be avoided. The problem child, bad report cards, and so on would disappear. Children would be trained in cooperation and later in life when social life appears, they would be able to contribute in cooperative ways.

Commentary:

The importance of family cannot be underestimated in Adler's psychology. The family is the social unit par excellence, "It is important for the future of the human race." Can anything stronger be expressed regarding the importance of family? Within the family cooperation is learned and practiced. Children grow up and pass on to another generation their knowledge and experiences of family. This makes the value of family most essential. Families must foster mutual respect, reason, contribution and cooperation. By doing so, they equip yet another generation with the resources necessary for survival. Children raised otherwise will be ill-equipped to govern their own behavior let alone raise responsible, cooperative children of their own.

17

Anxious Parents

This lecture was transcribed by Alan Porter. The date and occasion of this lecture are unknown. Dr. Adler talks about the parent's role within family and the importance of guiding children in socially useful ways with courage rather than anxiety.

Many parents are overburdened with fear. From the first day of a child's life, they watch over the child's behaviors with apprehension. They compare the child's actions with the actions of others whom they believe are normal. At the slightest difference they are shocked and alarmed. There are parents who are always trembling for their children. For these parents, when their children do anything which involves the slightest risk, the parents are paralyzed with fright.

It is good to be interested in a child's development. Parental interest in the child lays the foundation of the child's interest in other human beings. It is good to help children with their difficulties. No child could survive without the care of other people. But flutterings and anxieties were never any advantage. It is always best for parents to face a situation without tension, in full command of their faculties. We think best when we are level headed.

If parents are anxious, their children will be timid and self-centered. If we are always worrying, we cannot escape this. First born children and the "only" child suffer most from the anxiety of their parents. Parents of an "only" child are nearly always anxious. They want to guard the child from all dangers. They feel that if they lose this one child, they will lose everything. Every first child was once an only child. Moreover, with the first child, parents may feel their inexperience and wonder if they know enough to raise the child.

An exaggerated example of this anxiety was given by a peasant woman in Europe. She kept her son by her all his life. When he was fifty and she was seventy, they were both ill with pneumonia. The son was worse than the mother and had to be taken to the hospital. While he was there, he died. When the woman recovered from her illness, she was told of her son's death. She responded by saying "I always knew I would never raise that boy safely."

Now that we have so much advice on the physical and mental care of children, anxious parents have more opportunities to alarm themselves. All of our scientific knowledge is only applied common sense. There is no reason why parents should feel inferior. If they are courageous and independent themselves, if they are interested in their children, if they are willing to pick up parenting hints where they find them, if they are training their children to be courageous, independent, and interested in the welfare of others, the parents cannot make very big mistakes.

Even though I am an educator, I never like to put great emphasis on education in the home. It is bad for parents to have too many rules. It is bad for parents to always be warning or commanding their children. It is best for parents to be calm and confident in approaching their tasks. Parents should understand before everything else that children must learn to look after their own responsibilities without interference. Children should be given their own responsibilities. Children should be treated as equals. Every step in training children should be a step in independence.

If difficulties arise, it is of no use to attack the symptom. This is perhaps the greatest mistake in education. We should never concentrate on the symptom. We should consider what lies behind it. If a child lies and is afraid to tell the truth, the child does not trust other people. The child is not courageous enough. We cannot make the child tell the truth. We cannot force the child to be truthful. Perhaps the child has been afraid. We must help the child remove the reason for this. Our goal is to help the child find courage.

If a parent says, "My son is disobedient. How can I encourage him to obey me?" I have no golden rule in response to this. There are too many kinds of obedience. I can only say, "Do nothing, yet. Stop and look at why the child feels the need to disagree with you. Then you will remove the cause."

When children are disobedient, they do not like to cooperate with their parents. We cannot force children to like it. Children will not like cooperating with their parents wishes any more if we punish them. We must find out why these children are dissatisfied and why they revenge themselves in this way. It is not the disobedience that is important. It is the low interest in cooperation that matters. Punishment or long sermons on being a good child, will not change the behavior. The child has no interest in helping the parents. Perhaps the parents or others in the environment are making a mistake. The mistake must be corrected.

No difficulty calls for alarm. Instead, difficulties call for level-headed inquiry into their reasons and the removal of those reasons. Anxious parents will always be impatient and worry themselves to death over symptoms. The parent's anxiety reflects the parent's lack of confidence in themselves.

Commentary:

Adler advocates calm, level headed approaches to the challenges of parenthood. Parents have to teach children to trust others, to act with responsibility, and express interest in the welfare of others. This job is deterred when the parent's expressions of fear, anxiety and alarm surface. Parents are advised to examine parenting issues with rational means so that they can think through a useful course of action. Many difficulties can be avoided by calmly considering problem-solving strategies, rather than allowing feelings of anxiety to dominate actions. Children will learn to follow the lessons of reason and cooperation observed in their parents or children will learn less cooperative, more anxious ways of handling challenges.

18

The Importance of Mother

This speech was given at Temple Emanuel in New York City on November 12, 1929. Dr. Adler talks about the role of a mother within a family and society.

Individual Psychology does not say that women's place is in the home. It does empathically say that we cannot easily overestimate the importance of mothers' place in family life. It may not be necessary for the welfare of the human race that all women are mothers, but it is becoming increasing clear that society may expect great gains in the realm of human happiness when the role of motherhood is rightly understood.

It is not easy to lay aside old ways. The arduous tasks of housekeeping should not take away from the pleasurable aspects of homemaking. Perhaps we are not ready to accept the belief that women have a right to choose whether or not they will accept the responsibility of motherhood. Whether we accept this view or not, we can sympathize with the hope that one day all mothers will know the pleasure of raising their children and that homemaking will be raised to the high estate of a dignified profession.

Every mother is a teacher. She is the child's first interest. One of her tasks is to help the child gain interest in Father, siblings, and the larger society. If this task is performed well, the child will learn cooperation and will gradually grow in confidence and courage. When the child's parents have not learned cooperation themselves and the home is filled with quarreling, the child will not gain these skills.

The relationships of the mother are not simple. She has a relationship with the husband; she has a relationship with the child, and she has a relationship with society. We understand that none of these relationships can be over-stressed without damaging the others. If we focus solely on one relationship, the others suffer. We understand that in all of these relationships, a mother is bound in a harmonious way. In this way, she fosters cooperation and abilities of cooperation among her children. For instance, if a mother is focused on only one child, it is not enough. She must also foster the child's interest in the father. In turn, the father has to be receptive for this relationship to grow. If however, the mother fosters the child's interest in the mother only, the child will be resentful when asked to express interest in others. The child's ability for cooperation will be blocked. We see this with pampered children.

Mothers relationship to her husband must be such that the husband is willing to participate in building the child's cooperation. If mother and father are not able to cooperate, failures develop. If the child is illegitimate, if parents quarrel, if the parents divorce, the child does not gain the chance to cooperate with the parents. We can trace failure back to the child's early years when the mother's skills at building cooperation are essential. Later in life when the individual meets problems and challenges, the individual's ability to cooperate will be tested.

Preparation for motherhood must begin early in a girl's life. Boys and girls are not educated in an equal manner. Often in our culture, girls become disappointed in their future roles. It is important for girls to see their future roles with dignity. The family must overcome the superstition that boys are preferred and that girls are of minor importance. When parents express a preference for boys, girls become discouraged and dislike their future tasks. When these girls become mothers, they may resist their role. Women must be willing and prepare for this role.

Women resist motherhood when there are great difficulties. One great difficulty is impoverished social circumstance. We cannot overburden women. We have to improve the circumstances. We have to relieve the mother of economic duties so that she can fulfill the tasks of motherhood.

Some girls are not rightly prepared for motherhood. They have a mistaken view in this regard. They fear that they will be less attractive after giving birth to a child. They may also fear the child will be a rival for the husband's attention. These girls wish to be pampered. The best solution is an advisory council to assist the family with marital problems, questions of divorce, a lack of attention, etc. There are many mistaken views in married life that can be corrected so that married life can be improved. When couples are not taught cooperation, they follow their emotions and feelings. Their marriages fail and they always make mistakes toward the children. The couple is not rightly prepared for cooperation. We must educate them so that they understand the importance of cooperation.

In regard to the education of the child, the child's education begins when the child enters the world. The mother must be experienced and must not be brusquely astonished or surprised by the new situation she is now experiencing. She must know how to act toward the child and how to raise the child. In our society, traditions are followed. Sometimes those who are well intended but not well informed about child rearing, give child rearing advice. For instance, in family life, there must not be a supremacy. No one should be the most important member of the family. When this occurs, it must be remedied. Every family member can develop without the burden of the importance of another person.

You will find that parents and their children are living and growing like trees. If one of these grows quickly it damages the others. The mother must understand this. She must be aware that one child may develop better because mother used better methods and this child was better trained. It is dangerous for mothers to believe that one child is blessed or has inherited abilities that the other children do not have. When this occurs, we always find problems among the children. These problems can be avoided when the mother understands. If she does not prefer one child, she gives her love to each child. The love she has for her husband cannot be compared to the love she has for her children. It is wholly different.

The mother is in the best situation to identify with each of her children. She has raised each and must know each child's every expression and symptom. Sometimes a child is upset when the mother does not know the child's expressions and symptoms, but she should know. If the family grows and another child is born, the older children may be surprised. The mother has to prepare the older children for their new sibling. She must foster cooperation toward the new child. In this way, the older children will act as companions and friends with the newborn. If the older children prefer to be pampered, they will suffer. These are children who feel dethroned. They wish to fight and gain the attention they had before. In this fight the pampered child loses and becomes disliked, while the baby becomes more beloved. The more the child fights, the more the child is disliked. The child justifies fighting by blaming the mother for the time and attention she gives the baby.

The majority of failures in life are pampered children. It does not mean that the mother should not love this child, but she must not encourage the child to act dependent. The child has to be trained for social life. The mother has to consider the child's future. The mother has to understand social life. She must not be condemned to only housekeeping. She must participate and take part in her husband's business. Wives must understand these affairs because sometimes husbands die and widows are left helpless, this is a mistake.

No one should believe that I am saying women should not be educated for housekeeping. On the contrary, work must be satisfying. Women and men must develop on an equal level. Women must be encouraged to believe that they can be physicians, artists, etc. As long as they believe, they can compete. Some women block themselves and are too tense. They have the impression that the world is looking at them to see whether or not they can compete. Men have it easier. They do not worry if they are really able or not. This point must be stressed.

Housekeeping is not a lower task. It is a mistake to believe that it is a lower task. Men are guilty. Even in childhood, boys consider housekeeping as a task for servants. They believe that they are of a higher level and that they should not help Mother with housekeeping.

Mothers' work in the home is as great importance as the work of the father. Her work adds to his power. He can work much better if he is happy at home. Housekeeping can be done in a creative manner. We should not undervalue it. Women's activities outside the home should be increased. Women should have a broad field in which to perform. If they have an interest in a certain thing, they should not be stopped. They should be encouraged to pursue their interests.

In our culture it is a mistake to under value women and their work. This has the consequence that women resist and revolt against being undervalued. Devaluing women's contributions creates disharmony in the marriage. The woman's role in the family is not a lower role. There are no higher and lower roles. Everyone should be esteemed and cooperative. This is very important. Not only do men devalue the contributions of women, but you also find women who undervalue the contributions of women. In this way, women undervalue themselves.

If a mother under values her contributions, you will see the consequence. She may not feel equal to the father in education. She may say to the children, 'I'll tell your father…' This is a mistake. Children find the mistake, and they begin to rule and manage the mother. We are more educated by mothers than by fathers. It is a misperception that women do not educate. On the contrary, women have it easier as long as they can create cooperation. Her job is to raise the children so that they will be trusted. The mother and father must act as if they are comrades and friends. In this way they will gain esteem and cooperation. They must not use the authority that they are mothers and fathers. This practice is useless.

The development of the human race is in the hands of the mother. The child's inherited abilities or potentialities can be made useful when those abilities are trained in cooperation. The mother has to be skilled at listening and speaking. She has to be clear and to cooperate with the demands of society. A mother's greatest task is to understand social life as a whole and to participate in social life. In this way the child will be courageous about cooperating with others. The child will feel a sense of belonging.

If a child is an unwanted child, the child will not learn to get along with society. Therefore, the question of giving birth to a child is a very important one. We must console mothers if they do not agree with the role of motherhood. In a great many cases that I have seen, it happened that the mother wanted the child. When the mother wants the child, we can trust the tendency and attitude of the mother. After many investigations, we find that the tendency for mothers to protect their children is much greater than other instincts. It is much greater than the instinct for hunger. We can trust this tendency. We must not destroy it. In our society, the role of mother is seen as a lower role. We do not give mothers the credit they deserve.

The improvement of the human race resides in the field of social feeling. Social interest is the work of the mother. The mother is not only the pillar of the family and society, but the whole human race. If mothers fail, then our whole society is in danger. Therefore, mothers' role is very important. It is essential to help mothers understand their dignity, worth and value.

In the case of an unhappy marriage, the mother is not able to foster the child's interest in the father. If the parents disagree about the child's education, the quarrel pulls the child toward one side and damages the child. If the child is pampered by the mother and the father notices it and wants to change it, the result will be that the child resists the father and will be more connected to the mother. The parents must consent and find a way in which they can cooperate. Marriage is cooperation of two persons and cannot be solved by the rules one partner has in mind. It can only be solved in the rules of marriage and the education of the family.

Many of the failures in our society result from children brought up in orphanages where the mother cannot be replaced. Foster parents can replace the mother but cannot do more. Whatever we do to help these children, we cannot do anything more than find a replacement for the mother. All of the assertions that a child is better in an institution than in a home can only be explained by saying that we want the right type of mother. Rather than remove the child from the home, we might also find ways to help the mother succeed.

Individual Psychology is wholly in favor of helping the mother. We find ways to help the mother so that the child can act with cooperation. We understand the importance of the mother's role in fostering children's cooperation. When we look at the relationships of mother, father, child, and society, we see that the mother is the pillar of the whole social life.

Commentary:
Adler's advocates that mothers are the "pillar" of the family. This is no surprise. Her importance must be recognized and respected by everyone for its extraordinary value to society also. Adler ties the family role to that of society at large by stressing that a mother's role is of great value, and must be furthered in the minds of children and of society. He advocates equality for females and respects the individual rights of women to choose roles that suit them.

19

The Influence of the Father

This speech was given at Temple Emanuel in New York City on November 19, 1929. Dr. Adler talks about the role of a father within a family and society.

We know that the mother and the father have to cooperate. How is it that children see their father as an ideal for the whole of life and at other times they see him as an enemy? I will describe how a father ought to be. I want to remind you that the problems of fatherhood are not that different from the problems of motherhood. The father is not immediately connected or bound to the newborn. He has to contribute out of his experience and training. We cannot dethrone the mother. She always has been and must be the pillar of humanity. The father has to cooperate. To start a family, there must be cooperation between two persons. Individual Psychology offers us a good measure of an individual's ability to cooperate. We look at the individual's distance from the three life tasks. How does the individual approach society? If a man joins with others without hesitation and makes friends easily, this will influence his ability to cooperate in his marriage. He must be a part of the whole. It is a sign that he is adjusted to be a part of family life, to be a good husband and father. This is the first task of life. He must be a comrade and a friend. He must develop the characteristics of optimism and faith in others. He must be able to say yes to the human race. These are the traits of a socially adjusted individual.

In early childhood mothers train their children to be cooperative and socially adjusted. As men approach their occupations, the second life task, we see their level of cooperation. Men must be educated for occupation so that they will be able to support their families. In some families, the father will need his wife and children to assist him in supporting the family. In cooperation with his wife, he will teach the children to understand what is necessary in supporting the family. This is useful to the whole human race. It is important to be useful. To be a father, is to solve two problems of life with cooperation.

In regard to the third life task, namely the problem of love, we see comradeship. We see an individual making efforts to embellish his partner's life. This is the way a husband and father ought to behave. Sometimes I find that a father is able to cooperate, but his wife and children are working against him. The first step in remedying this situation is to go back to the man's courtship with his wife. You see, cooperation means equality. It does not mean that wives are servants. It does not mean that fathers rule the family which only fosters the notion of men's fictitious privilege. It does not mean that women are of a lower level because they do not have economic opportunities. Men should not forget that in accomplishing family life, the role of the woman cannot be surpassed and should not be undervalued especially in regard to financial matters. Husbands should never emphasize that they are economically superior, that money comes from him, or that he is supporting while others are accepting. Otherwise he will give the impression that his wife and children are of lower status and not equal.

Superiority and feelings of inferiority in the family must be avoided. If the wife is better educated, or comes from a family of higher social standing superiority, the husband's feelings of inferiority may arise. When this occurs, cooperation between husband and wife is replaced with compensation. The wife may elevate the husband while both partners strive for equality.

Fathers must be aware of social life. Men have it easier than women to experience social life. They have more freedom as children. Unfortunately in our society, men's sphere of activity is broader than women's sphere of activity. Men should not boast of this or abuse it. They should advise their wives and children as they would advise a friend.

When husbands and wives fight, the circumstances must be considered. A fight is always a defeat of the fighter, especially if the fighter is the husband. If the wife feels weaker and subjugated, she is stronger than her husband. In the family, the weaker is really the stronger. There is no advantage in a family fight.

I find that the way in which a man acts toward his parents and siblings will indicate his degree of cooperation. These relationships can be exaggerated and interfere with his own family life. This does not mean that he should dislike his parents and siblings. Indeed, he should esteem and love his parents and siblings. They should have good relations. Sometimes, parents become jealous of the new family and interfere. Persons must be educated for future social life. This will not occur if a husband or wife is leaning on his or her family of origin. Sometimes married men and women speak of home and mean the home of their parents. These individuals have not correctly joined their partner. This behavior may indicate a fight or a neurosis.

There should not be a fight between the families. Sometimes this happens when a man marries against his parents' wishes. Such a marriage is in danger, not because the parents saw things rightly, but because the parents create interference. It is necessary that a man understands what he must do. He must not look for the mistakes of his parents. If he can cooperate with his wife, danger can be avoided. Parents might antagonize before a couple marries, but after the marriage ceremony, parents should do everything to help the couple.

Parents should avoid showing children shyness, slyness and cunning. They are a sign that the individual hopes for an easier side of life. They also indicate that the individual is not courageous enough. Husbands and wives should have friends in the same society. It is a danger for them to have separate friends. If they go toward different sides, they are showing a lack of cooperation. That does not mean that they should cling to each other. Difficulty arises when husbands do not want their wives to be introduced in society. This is a mistake. Social life should not be decreased.

It is important for children to see that they are a part of society. It is essential for children to meet people outside of the family. Problems arise when fathers make their business life and their friends a secret. The father's social sphere and his interests should not be secretive. The children should be advised in all of these ways. These interests are of value to the whole human race.

Fathers should not use force or authority. He should be satisfied if he can explain and foster cooperation. This fact cannot be over stressed. If a child is found to be uncooperative, the child should not be punished. Corporal punishment is used in anger. There is no justice in it. It is used as revenge. When the child feels inferior, and always in the hand of the powerful father, the child's spirit of cooperation does not increase. Fathers' must not assume that educating the children is only the work of the mother. Fathers must participate in this task.

Love is wholly worthwhile when it is given with free will. Husbands do not have to show the children in a striking manner the affection they feel for their wives. When this occurs, children may feel that their place is narrowed, and they may pull back. Parents should not make a bagatelle out of sexual relations. In explaining sexual matters to their children, parents should explain only as much as the children can understand at their current level of development. Parents should not explain more, nor should they minimize their response to the children's questions.

One of the roles of fatherhood is to protect his wife and children. Fathers cannot show cowardice if the children are attacked. Children will long remember their parents acting cowardly and escaping their duties.

Husbands should not put heir wives in a dependent role. This will not be satisfactory. Cooperation is required in the household. Women who are not earning money independently of their husbands are sensitive to financial inequality. These wives are hurt when their husbands accuse them of extravagance. Finances should be settled in a cooperative manner and children should be advised about things that are affordable and things that are not affordable. Fathers should not believe that they can only secure their children's future with money. Fathers should not over stress the importance of money.

If a father wants his wife and children to do something, he has to look for their interest. When these interests are useful, the father should support them. It is not difficult to join the main interests of persons. There should not be a fight over a child's choice of occupation. Fathers should not boast of their success. If he really is successful, the children will look up to him. Children may be discouraged if their father is successful, and the children may feel that they cannot live up to their father's ideal. If the children work with their father, the father should not engage in competition with the children. He should let the children develop independently so that they feel worthwhile. If children develop an inferiority complex, they can easily be discouraged. Very good children can be very spoiled in that way. Fathers have to avoid favoring one child over another. If fathers show preference for the boys in the family over the girls, this can have damaging effects. Boys are always confronted to prove that they are more skilled than girls. On this point, boys meet the greatest difficulties.

There are times when one child develops more quickly than the others. It may be difficult not to show preference for this child. The father must be strong and experienced enough so that he does not show preference for one child over another. If the father indicates that this child is especially talented, the others will conclude that they are curtailed. The other children may express envy and jealousy. When children feel that they are equal, they can cooperate. Children must be taught that they are equal and they must experience equality. It is not enough to say they are equal. It has to be proven.

Jealousy is contrary to cooperation. It arises when one individual treats another like property. There is a reason for jealousy. It is the tendency of one person to rule another. Often jealousy is used to show superiority, to push another person, or to rule. For instance, if a father wants and likes to be high tempered and terrifies others he is intending that his wife and children should subjugate themselves to him. A Father should not be pedantic. If he is, he will give rules and look to see if the rules are being followed. It must be understood that rather than cooperate, he attempts to rule. Fathers must cooperate and they must teach their children to cooperate. If fathers fail at this, they will be faced with difficulties later in life because family members have not learned to cooperate. Later in life when the children have difficulty, they may say "my father was not a good father, so I did not develop rightly." This is not so. While every child has not made the mistake of failing to cooperate, it is much easier to develop a spirit of cooperation if the father has also cooperated.

Commentary:

In discussing the role of a father, Adler continues to promote cooperation as the means of meeting the challenges of fatherhood. He addresses the disadvantages related to male dominance within the family. Adler understands the importance of Father's ability to role model equality and cooperation. This is important between husband and wife. Family life educates children for future social behavior. Fathers must foster the feeling of courage and faith in positive outcomes. Fathers must work collaboratively with Mothers to promote cooperative endeavors while encouraging faith in positive outcomes.

20

Migraine

This lecture was given at the Long Island College of Medicine, Brooklyn, New York in January 1933. Dr. Adler talks about temperament and lifestyle as they relate to migraine headaches.

I have always found that migraine patients physically prepare themselves for fits of migraine. Throughout their lives they have expressed a certain degree of emotion and tension. Sometimes this is exaggerated. It is not true that these patients are always high strung. Nor is it true that symptoms arise from an emotional state of mind. There will always be high strung patients. Mental strain may run in the family. In a family where the father is temperamental, you may see a child who is temperamental. This patient may enter the office with a wild and angry face. This is a certain activity. These patients are active, but they do not express courage. Outbursts of temper betray an underlying inferiority complex.

Migraine patients are not sure that they can accomplish all that they want to accomplish. You will find migraine patients accomplish good things. However, they may believe that they can only accomplish certain things, if they terrify others. They do not understand that they can contribute and accomplish good things in a cooperative way. This does not mean that these individuals do not cooperate at all. It means they do not cooperate enough. Part of their activity is temperamental outbursts which are easy for them. You will also see that patients suffer migraines when they are free from this temper.

Temperamental outbursts express a hostile attitude toward life and toward the world. Migraine patients are hypersensitive. Acting as if they are living in enemy territory, hypersensitivity is the right stance and an intelligent characteristic for these individuals. This hypersensitivity is also a social trend. It is an attitude toward society. It is not heredity. It is a leading line that agrees with the whole style of life.

I find that migraine patients tend to be impatient. They want everything immediately. They cannot wait. If they have to wait, they feel hurt. They are easily hurt and offended. They tend to be highly sensitive to those who refuse to acknowledge their majesty. You see that migraine patients are very ambitious. They always want to be looked at, admired and worshiped, but in a different way. We must not use rules. We must not believe that diagnosis explains everything. We have to describe more. Each individual is different.

I call my psychology Individual Psychology because each person is different. If we see an individual who is acting high strung, you will see an inferiority complex or a superiority complex expressed in this way. To act temperamental and attempt to rule by temperamental outbursts, cannot be generalized by rules. It must be understood in terms of the individual. It is different in each case. Otherwise, you see, we would come to the standpoint which is expressed in this German proverb 'we would be in a dark night where all the cows are dark.' You see, on a dark night, everything is dark, everything is equal. We must not generalize in this way. We must get rid of this idea of equality. Generalizing is excluded more and more from Individual Psychology. Therefore, the use of the words Individual Psychology is wholly justified. This idea is not completely understood by the greatest part of this science.

While some highly temperamental people frequently experience migraines, you will also find that some highly temperamental people never experience migraines. Migraine sufferers are more interested in themselves than others. Therefore, treatment must encourage these patients to increase their interest in others. Each patient has his or her own problems. If an individual is married, it is possible that marriage and family life are problematic for the individual. The patient is always right. One migraine patient complained that her husband always came home from work tired and wanted to sleep. She was hurt and offended. Her migraines were a nonverbal expression of her emotions.

I see a certain degree of greediness among migraine sufferers. They are easily disappointed. They do not know what to do because they are afraid of being defeated. They want to excel, but they are hampered by their own fear of defeat. All these things can be observed in the migraine patient. The migraine is a neurosis. It only appears when there is a bodily readiness for it.

Commentary:
Headaches present complex symptoms, migraine headaches especially so. Strongly advocating the uniqueness of the individual, Adler explains that in order to understand the symptoms of migraine, one has to take into account the individual's life style. Once again we ask, what is the purpose of the symptoms? Many migraine sufferers

strive for perfection in haste, rather then suffer imperfection or perceived defeat, these individuals will suffer migraines. If they are encouraged to accept imperfections, it is likely that their headaches will ease.

21

The Problem of Crime

The date, occasion and transcription of this lecture are unknown. Dr. Adler talks about antisocial behavior. This lecture includes questions from the audience. Relative to crime prevention, Dr. Adler encourages parents and teachers to follow the guidelines of Individual Psychology in promoting social interest rather than self interest.

Let us look at crime. More than 40% of crimes are not detected. It must be confessed that we have not yet found a way to deal with crime successfully. This always means that something is not rightly understood. We do not want to say there will always be crime in such a high degree as we find it at present. An understanding of this complicated problem is most welcome.

The short time allotted for my speech must also be used to establish an understanding of Individual Psychology. It insists that life's main structure is to create, to go ahead, to develop, and to strive for success. How an individual relates to the outside world is seen in the individual's behavior. Heredity does not influence the individual's ability to strive in the right way. This cannot be taught from outside the environment. To strive in a more or less right way, is the creation of the individual. This is first seen in childhood. Everyone uses experience, education and environment in their own way as they relate to the outside world.

We cannot speak about types of criminals. We must go on and investigate the individual. How does the person relate to problems? We live in an environment that is limited by social demands. How does the individual look at life? How does the individual answer social demands? All of this is important. Everyone answers differently. These are the main views of Individual Psychology. We can build up the idea using views that are outside of our immediate experience. For speculation, using a metaphysical idea that is justified only after it appears, there is no contradiction of this idea from the experiences given to us.

Regarding the issue of striving for a personal success, there is no doubt that delinquents are always sure that in their deeds they will always find personal success. Delinquents utilize others. For the delinquent, others are merely objects. As we think about the way in which the delinquent relates to life, we have to ask, how did the delinquent come to the conviction that others are pawns? This question belongs to the science of Individual Psychology.

The delinquent has not developed the right ability to cooperate and contribute. From the beginning of this individual's life, the individual has not expressed high degrees of cooperation or contribution. This faulty attitude is not seen by everyone. For instance, I have seen a 15-year old boy who burglarized a store. His mother told me that among all her children, he had been the best child. It meant that he had been leaning on the mother, and that he had always gotten what he wanted, and that the mother was the type that humored the boy and did not find him a burden. This is an extreme case.

You will find that delinquents were of the "getting" type when they were younger children. They expected everything to be done by others, looking upon them like objects to be utilized. Everyone is property for delinquents, more or less, there are a million varieties.

Is delinquency formed by heredity or environment? We find delinquents among the best stock. We also find delinquents appearing in families where the children are less well-developed. There must be something more to it than heredity. The trouble arises when the child attempts to relate to life.

Which is more important: heredity or environment? Neither is important. Only the individual is important. The individual's ego, the individual's way of relating to self and others, the individual's goal in life and the way that the individual thinks about strength and weakness is important. We have no way to understand what heredity has to do with so called racial qualities. They have no direction because we always meet problems that our ancestors never met. The environment impresses each of us. The way that we respond to the environment results from our own creative power.

Education can do much, but it cannot predict. Delinquency cannot be predicted, but it can be seen in the first years if a child does not fit in the social environment and the child expresses low social interest for our complicated life. As long as a child does not feel a sense of belonging in the family, and as long as a child does not feel at home in the world, and as long as a child does not look for the solution of the problems of life, the child builds up an attitude toward the useless side of life. The child cannot verbalize it, but it is involved in the child's personality.

Another point which must be considered, if the child does not agree with demands from the outside, the child meets difficulties very early in life. The more pampered the child is, the more difficulties the child will meet. All delinquent children are a more active type in the beginning of life. They are critical, aggressive and they attack others. They always attack weaker people. They are always sure of their superior strength. They are vain, striving more and more for their personal success. They always want to be ahead of others, but not in a courageous way, which is the way of a socially adjusted person. We can see them escaping their problems very early in life. Even murders are sure of their conquest from the beginning in using weapons, or at least they believe themselves to be. They have a plan, but there is no courage, there is a slyness.

Plans of crime are probably formed long ago. This is marvelously described in Dostoevsky's, *Crime and Punishment*, where a student contemplates killing a woman usurer for two months because she cannot make use of her money. He cannot kill her for a long time. For two months, he trains to break down his social interest so he can kill her and have her money.

Inheritance of social interest cannot be destroyed, but it is not strong enough for our complicated life. It will not be successful unless it is cultivated. The student wants to have the property of the woman across the street. He asks himself something that is very interesting. He suddenly cries out, 'Am I Napoleon or am I a louse?' Then he gets up and kills the woman believing himself to be Napoleon. I see this fooling of one's self in each criminal case.

The case of a burglar was like a strong man who does not like to work. He said we do not know the terrible conditions of labor. For him and for many there is no place on this earth. He goes and kills because there is no place. To give all these comparisons is the way that delinquents justify themselves. Give them the possibilities for social interest. Perhaps they can behave differently. This is the same process that we find in poetry where people fool themselves by using metaphors that only explain in part.

Based upon their early failures to develop social interest, delinquents pick out something that helps them to find a release. This is a very important point because when delinquents are caught they are thinking, 'I have not planned rightly, and if I had not forgotten this or this I would not have been caught.' If imprisoned, the individual will say 'I did not succeed because I forgot some little thing.' 'If I had not forgotten my glasses,' said one criminal, 'I would not have been caught.'

Delinquents can only be changed if we help them increase their expressions of social interest. Someone must convince delinquents that they are capable of expressing more social interest. Until that is accomplished, our striving to diminish the number of crimes is fruitless. Nearly half of all delinquents coming out of prison repeat their crimes. This is because they have only private intelligence and not enough common sense. They act only in accordance with their delinquent aim, not for the improvement of human life. This must be changed before we can expect to deal rightly with crime.

Early in life, delinquents create their style of life with limited expressions of social interest. We must increase their expressions of social interest. The delinquent is always an active type. If failure develops for the passive type, it is usually seen as a neurosis, not delinquency. You must also consider that nearly normal persons have activity, but if a person has not developed social interest and is highly active, the individual will use this activity against others. This is what we call delinquency.

We must find an effective method to teach delinquents to increase their expressions of social interest in the right degree and to the right extent. Of course, the best and simplest way would be to teach all the parents, and to show all people how to bring up a child, and how to develop the child's expressions of social interest so that the child will not be a burden. I must say this task seems to me to be impossible.

I would like to teach parents as much as possible but I am not sure this would be sufficient. This would take a thousand years and then a million instructors. I would not recommend it. My collaborators and I do everything to teach the parents, but our method must be much stronger and more confident. Over the last twenty years, I have proposed that we could deal with the problem only if we could teach the teachers to encourage the child to express more social interest.

Children who have limited expressions of social interest, attack others. Teach children to behave in the right way, then we can hope that not only our generation but also the next generation will profit. Not only would we teach a large number of people how to behave, but this would spread over the whole country and all the parents would be told of the needs of such children. Therefore, this method would work immediately. It would mean that the school would be an instrument of social progress. Children who turn out to be criminals later in life are very often in a difficult situation in school. They hope to be personally successful. If children lose hope in school and they are active, then one must keep an eye on them. Imagine going regularly to a place where one is humiliated and where there is no hope.

I understand how many of these children have lost hope in school and hide themselves in places where they learn to lie, to amuse themselves and sometimes to become members of a criminal gang. Others teach them what to do. The first thing adults must do is to make it impossible for a child to feel hopeless in school.

How do we accomplish this? We begin by teaching teachers. No child should leave the school before the teacher is sure that the child has achieved a certain ability of cooperation and contribution. As it is now, we dismiss children who do not express cooperation and contribution and later find them in a reformatory or a prison.

Questions and Answers

I am often asked about the getting type. If one neglects a child, the child's desire to get what is missing will increase. Do you believe one can starve a child and this child will not then need more? If this type of an environment is very strong, the child will always appeal. It is a mistake to believe that the children in destitute homes cannot be pampered. I have seen people carry a child around all day in a destitute home. I have seen children cry and then get everything they want. Every time they opened their mouths, someone responded. We can train children so that they know that they can use the environment for their purposes.

How can we reform criminals? All systems can be worthwhile or worthless. It depends upon how the delinquent can be changed. To train delinquents is not enough. I do not believe that keeping them in prison is the only way. We need to devise ways of convincing these individuals that they are wrong. Then they would need to learn Individual Psychology.

Do politics and economics affect the crime rate? Crimes are often attributed to economics and politics but each crime results as a failure to meet a certain problem. Criminals are not prepared to solve a social problem. Problems increase when there are economic and political difficulties. As the price of food increases, the number of crimes increases. Even in times of prosperity, with rising prices, crimes increase. If economic conditions become worse, the number of crimes increases. The less social interest people express, the more likely they are to become delinquents and criminals.

Why do wealthy people steal? Many wealthy people gain pleasure in stealing. It is a feeling of success like gambling or fraud. Someone exploits someone else. We have no law against it. Our social interest is not so sensitive. Our inherited interest is not sufficient.

Some people believe that if you give everyone what they want, they will not steal. This is commonplace. A rich man will not be a pickpocket, but I do not want to speak of commonplace matters. Individuals may be tested in ways for which they are not prepared. They may be tested to such a high degree that they may not meet the demands of the situation.

Up to now I have not found any contradictions to my explanation of crime. I am often asked 'Does a high IQ have any relation to crime?' If feeble minded or insane persons commit something, I do not call those acts, crimes. Only when intelligent people commit crimes would I call those acts, crime. They look upon the world and believe it is their property. There are different I.Q.'s among delinquents. The most intelligent are the burglars. They are very intelligent and sly. The others have not such a high IQ.

We find that 50% of all delinquents suffer from sexual illnesses. They have made love their personal pleasure. It is not common sense and would not be accepted as such. You find them failing in all the great problems of life. They cannot join with other people. They cannot join honest persons without exploiting them. They can defend each other and have a certain honor among themselves. There is a certain amount of social interest. The degree of social interest cannot be diminished but it can be increased.

How can society set about re-educating adults who are criminals? I have done a great deal of it, and it is the only way to deal with those on social welfare. If I explained it to you, I would have to use a case. If you understand that criminals relate themselves in a mistaken way to the problems of life, you may be able to help them understand this. I do not know if you will always succeed, but the more they are trained in this approach, the more success we will have.

No one can force individuals to increase their expressions of social interest. Everyone has always said it should be, but this is not sufficient. There is a certain art to it. I cannot explain everything that I have found out, but I will do so shortly. One must give individuals the chance to feel successful in a socially interested way. It belongs to what I have said in the beginning of my lecture. Individuals are always striving for success. If an individual finds it a success to destroy things, or the individual takes advantage of others, give this person a chance to be successful in a socially interested way. One person can do it. Another cannot. Many teachers can do it. Perhaps we find a great number of persons who can do it.

We see social interest among animals, among bees. Buffaloes defend themselves against wolves. You never find an isolated person unless he or she is insane. Therefore, all of us are built up to conform to society. We all learn how to look, how to listen, and how to speak. People are only rightly developed if they express enough social interest. For instance, what do you think is the highest expression, to think or to conclude. We know that everyone has to think; we will have to think for eternity. The first act which nature provides for the child, is the relationship with the mother. Both are built up by nature for cooperation. Mothers' love is a part of social interest.

Commentary:
Adler introduces social interest in his remarks on crime. This comes from the German word gemeinshaftsgefühl which is more literally expressed as community feeling. However, social interest is more frequently used. Community feeling or social interest exists within each person, but needs to be nurtured to develop. From this comes a willingness to cooperate by recognizing that we are all part of the cosmos. We must share and cooperate. The criminal seeks to avoid these matters by self-serving behavior.

Criminals want to shortcut the work of problem-solving. They feel entitled to special consideration. Others should serve them as objects for their use. Their actions demonstrate how they feel. Lacking the strength and willingness to problem-solve the tasks of life by individual responsibility and cooperation, criminals believe that exploitation of others is the only way they can achieve success. Given their misperceptions, taking advantage of others is the only way they know how to participate.

22

Death

The date, occasion and transcription of this lecture are unknown. Dr. Adler talks about children's reactions to death and explains how to help children understand death. He mentions Freud's Death wish and explains how Individual Psychology has a different view of death.

Little is known about the ways in which young children are affected by coming into contact with death. There is more than one answer to this question. Undoubtedly, once a child's lifestyle has become fixed, a very decisive difference occurs in the child's reaction to death. Prior to the establishment of the lifestyle, any impression the child has of death is similar to the child's impression of the disappearance of a person or thing. Such disappearances are, of course, common experiences in the life of a child. Death teaches a child to form conclusions about disappearance. The child does this in accordance with his or her personal discretion and learns to reckon with the fact that people and things are capable of disappearing.

Once the life style is formed and the child has assumed a definite attitude toward the problems of life, a very different state of affairs comes into being. Then, death, or the sight of a dead person, are summed-up, assimilated and responded to in accordance with the dictates of the lifestyle. As with an adult, the child's ability to accept the fait accompli is decided by the child's lifestyle. For instance, an individual expressing a pampered lifestyle, with an all or nothing subjective outlook, is generally susceptible to suffering and will react in all manner of ways.

The pampered lifestyle is the personal creation of a neglected child, or the child who feels neglected. The most important factor regarding death is the degree of attachment that existed between the child and the deceased. If the child did not like the deceased, or the deceased stood between the child and a third person or something the child wanted, the child may react to the death with genuine satisfaction. A wise counselor will determine whether the child regards the death as eternal or merely a transitory disappearance. The counselor will also attempt to understand the extent to which the death strikes the child as a profound occurrence or a serious matter for the deceased, as well as, the environment.

The child's realization of the inevitability of death produces various reactions. These reactions vary in accordance with the individual's life-style. Every human being understands the fact that life on earth is not everlasting. Suicide and disguised forms of suicide such as insanity and drug addiction are more or less active responses to the alleged obstructions in life. They are hindrances that prevent conformation to the laws of living.

A distorted lifestyle is blocked in its striving to master the three main problems of life. Here, we see individuals sensing that their whole existence is endangered. For healthy individuals the consequent shock effects are overcome. Shock effects are retained by less healthy individuals as alleviating alibis. The fear of death comes within this sphere of shock reactions and appears because all hope of solving the menacing problem seems to have been deterred. For example, a five-year-old boy was spanked by his Aunt. He screamed at the top of his lungs and shouted 'How can I go on living when you degrade me like that?' In later life he developed melancholia and filled his mind with thoughts of death and suicide. Another child was not allowed to go out and play with other children. This child spent his time alone in his room or with his governess. Upon the news of his father's death, the child ran to his governess and asked: 'Now, may I go out and play?'

For the neurotic patient, the threat of defeat is a violent shock. It is a menace to the individual's vanity and prestige. This individual's hypersensitive self suffers shock as intensely as if it were the hand of death. Going one step further, the neurotic patient views death as the only hope for avoiding loss of prestige. These individuals toy with the idea of suicide and the desire to die.

For a long time Freud indicated this death wish in his patient's dreams. He always related the death wish to his misconception of the sexual libido and the inherited destructive drive. Freud ignored the fact that the potential neurotic patient, the child who is likely to behave neurotically as an adult, is egotistical and expresses an alien notion of reality. This individual lives a strongly defensive life, is hypersensitive and overly emotional. In the end, this individual blindly arrives at the trained failure of passive resistance (See Adler, A. *Aggressionstrieb in der Neurosis*, 1908 and Adler, A. *Uber den Nervosen Charakter*, 1912).

Once neurotic patients have an alibi in the form of symptoms, they will focus on those symptoms. This prevents the neurotic patients from overcoming problems, while they preserve their prestige and strive for significance. The problem of death retreats into the background, remaining in the person's mind, where it may be called upon at some point in the future, depending on the person's lifestyle. Sometimes it is fairly clearly present, at other times, it is less apparent.

It must not be imagined that the suffering of the neurotic patient is unreal; it is very real indeed, and often exaggeratedly so. This suffering forms an effective guard against a loss of prestige. It is a general error in psychiatric literature to speak as though the patient made a deliberate escape into neurosis; as though the patient were fond of the symptoms and did not wish to give them up. The very contrary is the case: the neurotic patient would gladly surrender the symptoms, if the individual were not threatened by the greater of the two evils: thoughts of death and the loss of prestige. Real death means the end of the striving for a successful solution. The significance of corporal death is that it brings with it an end of striving for a successful solution to the problems of life. Spiritual death, particularly for the neurotic patient, is no less terrifying.

For example, a thirty-year-old teacher who had been married for six months, lost her job during the great depression. Her husband was also out of work. Against her will, she accepted a job as a clerk. Every day she took the subway to work. One day she became obsessed with the fear that if she didn't get up from her seat at once, she would die. Some of her fellow workers took her home, where she recovered from her anxiety. Thereafter, when she was in the subway, she would be seized with terrible thoughts of sudden death. It became impossible for her to go on with her job.

It was not difficult to get a general idea about this case. The individual's movements are of utmost interest. They are explicable forms of individual expression. For example, stuttering is a movement that is interpreted as a hesitating movement. In this case, looking at the patient's movements and ignoring the thought content of her anxiety and obsession with death, it is clear that her movement is successful. She moved from a point that she found humiliating, to one that somehow served to protect her against the fear of defeat. Her thought content explains that she found her job degrading. It represented a complete moral defeat. This reveals a great deal about the patient's lifestyle and her understanding of life. This woman was vain and haughty, she was extremely self-conscious, inactive and her expressions of social interest were minimal. In short, she has one of the varieties of the pampered lifestyle.

The patient was the second of three children. She had an older sister and a younger brother. Second born children are known for their efforts to outstrip the older child. This patient was true to type. She described her father as cantankerous. Her sister could never get anything out of him, while the patient was always able to do so, usually by crying.

Crying is the medium known as water power. It is a weapon of the weak, fairly inactive person and who gains success through the weakness of others. By the use of water power, the patient managed to feather her own nest at her sister's expense. When her sister was given a ring by the mother for doing well on a school exam, the patient didn't stop crying and begging until she had a ring as well.

The woman's younger brother was a strong rival. While the father paid little attention to his wife and daughters, he made a great favorite of his son. The parent's marriage was unhappy. This fact shocked the patient and led her to harp strongly on the neglectful nature of the male sex.

When she was asked if her own marriage was a happy one, she burst into tears and declared herself the happiest woman alive. I asked her if this happiness was anything to cry about, and she answered that she always feared the marriage would end on an unhappy note. She was wrought up over every kind of defeat, real or imagined. Obviously, the goal she had in mind (unknown to herself) was to establish her superiority and security by instinctively presenting herself as a person who was easily shocked and depended upon the soft-heartedness and indulgence of others. Thus, like all neurotics, she was the type who has little interest in the welfare of other people, prefers to regard them as objects of exploitation and displays very limited activity.

Between herself and the job she found so degrading she interjected the death problem as a safeguard. That is to say, the death problem interjected itself when the patient found herself robbed of every chance of success. (Note, Many critics imagine that we hold neurotic individuals personally responsible for their symptoms and suffering. This misunderstanding arises through the failure to appreciate the inadequacy of language. Because the Individual Psychologist succeeds in grasping the neurotic situation, the critics assume that the patient has grasped it too. We must say that neurotic individuals cannot be held responsible until they have grasped the truth of the situation. We say the same for the critics.)

In this respect, the woman's dreams were of great interest. When asked about her dreams, she always reported images with dead people. Anyone with a knowledge of the Individual Psychological interpretation of dreams might guess that she would dream in this way. Her lifestyle was obliged to select such images so that death images were reinforced by her dreams. Her dreams intensified her terrifying fear of death because they served as a poignant training in the demands of her lifestyle. Her neurotic attitude can be simply and succinctly described. She seems to say: 'Better to die than to go on with this job.' In analysis this means not death at all, but the throwing-up of a job.

What this woman understood about her condition was a number of disconnected, isolated facts. She understood nothing about the coherent whole, the totality, composed of her life form, her conception of life and the exogenous factor. Some people would call this unrealized coherence, the unconscious. In that case, it must be in the unconscious minds of all who fail to understand it.

Commentary:
Death is a part of life. Many adults avoid talking about it with children. Consequently, children are confused and misinformed about death. It is possible that the topic creates discomfort for adults. These feelings of discomfort inhibit communication and the sharing of beliefs. Avoiding the issue only compounds confusion. Silence creates mystery. Rather than convey confusion and discomfort, many adults fail to convey to children meaningful information regarding death. Adults must find the courage to risk discomfort so that they can help children face the challenges of living and dying.

23

Psychological Aspects in a Time of Economic Crisis

While this lecture occurred in the first part of the last century, its message is valuable to today. We are not aware of the circumstances surrounding its presentation.

The only test for an individual's style of life and its meaning in a certain situation is the degree of social interest. Good, bad, normal, abnormal, right, wrong, intelligent stupid, etc. always express social relations. From a second point of view, but also as social relations, we have to consider the degree of activity in attitudes like daring, courageous, timid, contributing, exploiting, hurrying, procrastinating, shy, arrogant, reserved, etc. The main factor to consider in the science of psychology is social relations toward external problems: social because of their value for the welfare and progress of the human race.

In difficult situations the style of life becomes much more apparent. We find part of society coping with difficulties, struggling more or less in the ways of cooperation, stopping, blocking; one part optimistic, the other pessimistic. Either part can behave in a more active or more passive way: leading, acting, sometimes counteracting within their own ranks; or cowed down, apparently submissive, secretly resentful. Like the medical psychologist, the Individual Psychologist, has to contend with those who express a faulty activity or those who have fallen into a dangerous passivity. Sooner or later both reach their limits and express a low degree of social interest. Both types depart from cooperation by means of active or passive behavioral expressions. Those less active are inclined to develop a neurosis or psychosis that gives them seeming success, but is only an alibi, an excuse. They appeal to the help of others, or they desert all social problems and escape through suicide. In clinics, the increase of people who feel the general economic crisis is their own personal tragedy, and who experience a disturbed family life, and who have trouble with love and marriage problems, is striking. To be fair, it must be emphasized that economic difficulties also exist that are too heavy a burden for the greater part of humanity.

Extreme economic problems can be relieved only by social reconstruction. Many passive people become the prey of more active leaders who themselves are not well adjusted socially. Those who are passive become obedient servants while the active leaders only promote frenzied followers. It is interesting to observe in the evolution of the human race, that the active leader can only find followers in the name of social interest when group egotism is fostered. In any case this passive segment—socially fitted or not—follows a leader who convinces the group through the leader's own triumphs of the possibility of success. This gives mass movements their form.

To a large segment of the people, who are more easily discouraged because they lack the right degree of social interest, the future looks dark. For these individuals, confidence in others decreases and life seems to be futile. Hopelessness, the greatest danger for individuals as well as the masses, grows. Social feeling, as in a panic, is at an end. Government assistance and private help, unavoidable as a means of emergency relief, cannot replace the joy of life, or of work, or of hope in the future. Many persons feel degraded through no fault of their own. Resentment increases. The horrible torture of unoccupied time and the futile search for work, often give enticement to different subversive, wanton, unsocial efforts.

People who display an expecting, exploiting style of life, from childhood onward have enjoyed a great deal of unsocial activity. They are nearer to delinquency in a time of crisis than ever before. These individuals are likely to engage in crimes of all sorts. Thus, criminal activity increases.

Times of economic crisis are tests for the individual as well as society. It is a grilling examination regarding the degree of cultivated social interest. The inherited and acquired social feeling may not be strong enough to enable the individual to achieve a useful way of cooperating with society. The crisis produces, as in a panic, too much neglect, hatred, distrust, despair, and collapse in education, science, art, culture, social life, work, and in the relation among the sexes.

Only those members of society who are socially adjusted from childhood, and those who are active in their struggle for social progress, can stand the test of these difficulties and will succeed sooner or later. Their attitude is that not only do the advantages of social life belong to everybody, but also all the disadvantages. The latter must be solved for the benefit of the human race. To the psychologist and to the psychiatrist, a time of extreme economic crisis with all its misery gives a clearly expressed hint about how much has been neglected in the education of our generation and how much more must be accomplished for future generations.

Commentary:
Adler addresses the economic crisis that occurred in the late 1920's and early 1930's. It is likely that this speech was given after the Stock Market on Wall Street crashed in October 1929. Germany had been an economic leader prior to World War I. After the war, Germany suffered harsh economic reparations. Economic difficulties were experienced throughout Europe. The great depression of the 1930's was about to hit.

Economic hardship such as these tax individuals and society. Such times bring out the best and the worst in people. Each manifestation reflects the unique lifestyle of the individual. Times of stress and strain do not bring about changes in an individual's coping style. It may however, require greater resolve to express social interest and cooperation. A crisis is a challenge to mobilize resources. In times of crisis, healthy individuals will act in accordance with what is good for all. These individuals promote social interest and community feeling. Social and economic challenges may try our souls, but they also build bridges among us.

References and Additional Reading

Adler, A. (1908). Der Aggressionstrieb im Leben und in der Neurose. *Fortschritte der Medizin, 26,* 577–584. (Reprinted in Heilen und Bilden, 1914, Munich: Reinhardt).

Adler, A. (1978) Cooperation Between the Sexes. Garden City, New York: Anchor Books.

Adler, A. (1930) The Education of Children. New York: Greenberg.

Adler, A. (1949) Guiding the Child. London: Allen & Unwin.

Adler, A. (1914) Life-Lie and Responsibility. In: Practice and Theory of Individual Psychology. Totowa, NJ: Littlefield, Adams & Company.

Adler, A. (2002) *The Neurotic Character.* San Francisco, CA: The Classical Adlerian Translation Project. (Originally published in German in 1912, Uber den Nervosen Charakter. Wiesbaden: Bergman. The Neurotic Constitution. New York: Dodd, Mead & Company).

Adler, A. (1930) The Pattern of Life. New York: Cosmopolitan Book Company.

Adler, A. (1925) The Practice and Theory of Individual Psychology. Totowa, NJ: Littlefield.

Adler, A. (1963) The Problem Child. New York: Capricorn Books.

Adler, A. (1964) Problems of Neurosis: A Book of Case Histories. New York, NY: Harper Torch Books.

Adler, A. (1929) The Science of Living. New York: Greenberg.

Adler. A. (1939) Social Interest: A Challenge to Mankind. New York: G.P. Putnam Sons.

Adler, A. (1907) The Study of Organ Inferiority and its Physical Compensation: A Contribution to Clinical Medicine. New York: Moffat-Yard.

Adler, A. (1979) Superiority and Social Interest. New York: Norton.

Adler, A. (1927) Understanding Human Nature. New York: Greenberg.

Adler, A. (1929) Alfred Adler: Fox Movietone Newsreel Clip

Adler, A. (1931) What Life Should Mean to You. New York: Blue Ribbon Books.

Adler, K. & D. Deutsch (1959) Essays in Individual Psychology. New York: Grove Press.

Ansbacher, H. & R. (1956) The Individual Psychology of Alfred Adler: A Systematic Presentation in Selections of His Writings. New York, NY: Basic Books.

Bottome, P. (1939) Alfred Adler: the Man and His Work. New York: G.P. Putnam Sons.

Brett, C. (1998) Social Interest: Adler's Key to the Meaning of Life. Oxford, England: Oneworld Publications.

Brett, C. (1998) Understanding Life. Central City, MN: Hazeldon.

Brett, C. (1998) What Life Could Mean to You. Central City, MN: Hazeldon.

Dinkmeyer, D.C.; Dinkmeyer, D.C. Jr.; & L. Sperry (1987) Adlerian Counseling and Psychotherapy. Columbus, OH: Merrill Publishing.

Dostoyevsky, Fyodor (1917) Crime and Punishment. New York: P.F. Collier & Son.

Dreikurs, R. (1953) Fundamentals of Adlerian Psychology. Chicago: Alfred Adler Institute.

Dreikurs, R. (1967) Psychodynamics, Psychotherapy and Counseling. Chicago: The Alfred Adler Institute.

Eckstein, D. & R. Kern (2002) Psychological Fingerprints Lifestyle Assessments and Interventions. Dubuque, IA: Kendall/Hunt Publishing Company.

Emerson, R. W. (1859). Essays. Boston: Philips Sampson and Co.

Freud, S. (1930). Civilization and its Discontents. London: The Hogarth Press, Ltd.

Griffith, J. & R. Powers (1984) An Adlerian Lexicon Chicago: America's Institute of Adlerian Studies.

Hoffman, E. (1994) The Drive for the Self: Alfred Adler and the Founding of Individual Psychology. Reading, MA: Addison-Wesley Publishing.

Manaster, G. & R. Corsini (1982) Individual Psychology: Theory and Practice, Itasca, IL: F.E. Peacock Publishers.

Montagu, A. (1970). Social Interest and Aggression Potentialities. Journal of Individual Psychology, *26* (1), 17–31.

Mosak, H. (1977) On Purpose. Chicago, IL: Alfred Adler Institute.

Orgler, H. (1963) Alfred Adler, the Man and His Work. London: Sidgwick & Jackson.

Powers, R. & J. Griffith Understanding Life-Style: The Psycho-clarity Process. Chicago: America's Institute of Adlerian Studies.

Rom, P. (1975) Alfred Adler's Individual Psychology and its History. London: Adlerian Society of Great Britain.

Shulman, B. (1973) Contributions to Individual Psychology. Chicago: Alfred Adler Institute.

Shulman, B. & H. Mosak (1985) Manual of Life-Style Assessment. Muncie, IN: Accelerated Development.

Sperry, L. & J. Carlson (1994) Psychopathology and Psychotherapy: From Diagnosis to Treatment. Muncie, IN: Accelerated Development.

Stone, M. H. (1997a). Ibsen's Life-lie and Adler's Lifestyle. Individual Psychology, *53* (3), 322–330.

Stone, M. H. (1997b). Ibsen and His Feelings of Inferiority. The Canadian Journal of Adlerian Psychology, *27*, (1), 73–84.

Stone, M. H. (2002) Life Lies and Self Deception. Chicago: Phaneron Press.

Sweeney, T. (1981) Adlerian Counseling: Proven Concepts and Strategies. Muncie, IN: Accelerated Development.

Way, L. (1956) Alfred Adler: An Introduction to His Psychology. London: Pelican Books.

Index

A

Addiction. *see also* Alcoholic
Adolescents 37, 52, 59, 60
Aggression 11, 111
Alcoholic 2, 6, 34, 43
Anxiety 7, 35, 43, 56, 77, 79, 103
Avoidance 41

B

Behavior 6, 17, 18, 39, 41, 47, 49, 57, 62, 72, 73, 74, 76, 78, 87, 90, 94, 100
Birth Order 35, 72, 73, 76, 81, 102
Blushing 41
Bulimia 42, 44, 45

C

Common Sense 11, 28, 33, 34, 48, 78, 97, 99
Community Feeling. *see also* Social Interest 2, 9, 20, 21, 26, 27, 28, 29, 44, 48, 55, 56, 68, 84, 94, 95, 96, 97, 98, 99, 100, 103, 106, 107, 108, 109, 110, 111
Compensation 19, 62, 87, 110
Cooperation 2, 3, 5, 6, 7, 8, 9, 14, 28, 29, 31, 32, 35, 41, 49, 50, 51, 53, 54, 57, 58, 59, 63, 64, 66, 68, 69, 70, 71, 73, 75, 76, 78, 79, 80, 81, 82, 83, 84, 86, 87, 88, 89, 90, 95, 98, 100, 106, 108, 109
Courage 28, 29, 30, 31, 32, 33, 34, 35, 39, 45, 50, 51, 52, 53, 58, 59, 65, 69, 75, 77, 78, 80, 90, 91, 96, 105
Creativity 17, 24, 29
Crime 94, 96, 97, 98, 99, 100, 110

D

Delinquency 95, 97, 107
Detour 2, 48, 52
Discouragement 6, 7, 30, 31, 62
Dreaming 4, 7, 41, 102, 104, 105

E

Education 1, 3, 5, 17, 26, 30, 33, 34, 39, 48, 50, 51, 52, 60, 75, 78, 81, 83, 84, 94, 95, 107, 108, 109
Ego 12, 13, 14, 15, 17, 20, 95
Emotions 4, 7, 25, 56, 67, 69, 81, 92
Encouragement 27, 35, 53
Equality 34, 62, 64, 65, 69, 71, 72, 85, 87, 89, 90, 92
Excuses 34

F

Failure 7, 8, 31, 32, 35, 41, 47, 81, 97, 98, 102, 104
Family 3, 7, 10, 27, 38, 41, 42, 48, 49, 52, 55, 62, 64, 65, 71, 72, 73, 75, 76, 77, 80, 81, 82, 83, 84, 85, 86, 87, 88, 89, 90, 91, 92, 95, 106
Fear 32, 35, 38, 40, 41, 46, 56, 64, 73, 77, 79, 81, 92, 102, 103, 105
Fiction 64
Freud, Sigmund 17

G

Goals vii, 3, 4, 5, 7, 9, 12, 13, 17, 20, 25, 26, 28, 29, 32, 33, 35, 39, 40, 44, 47, 49, 55, 57, 64, 67, 68, 71, 78, 95, 104
Guilt 13, 15

H

Happiness 29, 39, 40, 68, 80, 104
Hopelessness 107
Human nature 69, 72, 110
Human race 2, 3, 4, 5, 9, 14, 15, 22, 26, 32, 35, 67, 68, 69, 71, 75, 76, 80, 83, 84, 86, 88, 106, 107

I

Id 12, 14, 15, 17
Immortality 2
Impatience 5, 6
Imperfections 5, 6, 45, 93
Inferiority feelings 16, 20, 27
Inheritance. *see also* Heredity
Intelligence 13, 27, 28, 51, 55, 61, 97

J

Jealousy 74, 89

L

Life tasks 9, 86
Lifestyle 44, 91, 101, 102, 103, 104, 105, 108, 111
Lying 52, 58

M

Marriage. *see also* Tasks of Life, Life tasks
Masculine protest 16
Misbehavior 26, 74
Montagu, Ashley ix
Motivation 48
Movement 9, 11, 17, 20, 25, 26, 29, 103

N

Neglected child 27, 101
Neurosis 27, 41, 56, 87, 92, 97, 102, 103, 106, 109
Normal 2, 6, 13, 36, 39, 77, 97, 106

O

Oedipus 13, 14, 16, 19

Optimism 7, 9, 18, 86
Organ inferiority 110

P

Pain 24, 25, 31
Parenting 36, 78, 79
Perception 66
Perfection 44, 45, 68, 93
Personality 9, 12, 13, 17, 24, 26, 95
Perversion 13
Power 3, 4, 9, 11, 13, 15, 20, 24, 40, 65, 67, 74, 83, 95, 104
Pride 16, 28
Psychosis 41, 106

R

Reason 25, 32, 35, 38, 44, 49, 58, 76, 78, 79, 89
Resistance 43, 44, 54, 56, 102
Revenge 16, 46, 78, 88

S

Security 104
Self-confidence 33, 34, 39
Self-esteem 30
Siblings 17, 62, 80, 87
Social Interest 2, 9, 20, 21, 26, 27, 28, 29, 44, 48, 55, 56, 68, 84, 94, 95, 96, 97, 98, 99, 100, 103, 106, 107, 108, 109, 110, 111
Society 2, 22, 23, 26, 27, 28, 31, 33, 35, 43, 47, 58, 61, 63, 64, 66, 69, 70, 73, 80, 82, 83, 84, 85, 86, 87, 88, 91, 99, 106, 107, 108, 111
Socrates 14
Stealing 98
Striving 4, 5, 6, 7, 10, 11, 12, 13, 16, 19, 20, 24, 25, 28, 29, 39, 44, 46, 48, 49, 55, 67, 68, 69, 71, 72, 74, 94, 96, 99, 102, 103
Success 5, 31, 32, 38, 40, 41, 43, 46, 51, 68, 89, 94, 95, 96, 98, 99, 100, 104, 106, 107

Suffering 5, 6, 23, 25, 27, 39, 40, 44, 101, 103, 104
Suicide 2, 16, 20, 23, 34, 52, 102, 106
Superiority 4, 5, 6, 7, 8, 9, 16, 19, 20, 25, 26, 28, 29, 34, 46, 49, 54, 64, 69, 72, 87, 89, 92, 104, 110
Sympathy 24
Symptoms 6, 11, 12, 21, 25, 37, 42, 44, 55, 56, 79, 82, 91, 92, 103, 104

U
Unconscious 10, 12, 14, 15, 17, 19, 105
Unity 4, 7, 26, 34, 52, 69

V
Virtue 3, 22

W
Watson, John 5

0-595-31144-X

Made in the USA
Lexington, KY
13 February 2014